SPECIMENS OF
BUSHMAN FOLKLORE

Copyright © 2007 BiblioBazaar
All rights reserved

Original copyright: 1911,
LONDON

W. H. I. Bleek and L. C. Lloyd

SPECIMENS OF BUSHMAN FOLKLORE

EDITED BY THE LATTER
WITH AN INTRODUCTION BY
GEORGE McCALL THEAL

BIBLIOBAZAAR

SPECIMENS OF
BUSHMAN FOLKLORE

TO ALL FAITHFUL WORKERS.

CONTENTS

PREFACE. 15
INTRODUCTION. 23

A. MYTHOLOGY, FABLES, LEGENDS, AND POETRY

THE MANTIS ASSUMES THE FORM OF A
    HARTEBEEST. 37
!GAUNU-TSAXAU (THE SON OF THE MANTIS),
    THE BABOONS, AND THE MANTIS. 43
THE STORY OF THE LEOPARD TORTOISE. 51
THE CHILDREN ARE SENT TO THROW THE
    SLEEPING SUN INTO THE SKY. 53
THE ORIGIN OF DEATH; PRECEDED BY A PRAYER
    ADDRESSED TO THE YOUNG MOON. 58
THE MOON IS NOT TO BE LOOKED AT WHEN
    GAME HAS BEEN SHOT. 62
THE GIRL OF THE EARLY RACE, WHO
    MADE STARS. 64
THE GREAT STAR, !GAUNU, WHICH, SINGING,
    NAMED THE STARS. 67
WHAT THE STARS SAY, AND A PRAYER TO A STAR. 68
!KO-G!NUING-TARA, WIFE OF THE
    DAWN'S-HEART STAR, JUPITER. 70
THE SON OF THE WIND. 76
THE WIND. 79
#KAGA'RA AND !HAUNU, WHO FOUGHT EACH
    OTHER WITH LIGHTNING. 82

THE HYENA'S REVENGE. First Version 85
THE HYENA'S REVENGE. Second Version 87
THE LION JEALOUS OF THE VOICE OF
    THE OSTRICH. 88
THE RESURRECTION OF THE OSTRICH. 92
THE VULTURES, THEIR ELDER SISTER,
    AND HER HUSBAND. 95
DDI-XERRETEN, THE LIONESS,
    AND THE CHILDREN. 99
THE MASON WASP AND HIS WIFE. 102
THE YOUNG MAN OF THE ANCIENT RACE,
    WHO WAS CARRIED OFF BY A LION;
    WHEN ASLEEP IN THE FIELD. 103
A WOMAN OF THE EARLY RACE AND
    THE RAIN BULL. 110
THE GIRL'S STORY; THE FROGS' STORY. 113
THE MAN WHO ORDERED HIS WIFE TO
    CUT OFF HIS EARS. 116
THE #NERRU AND HER HUSBAND. 117
THE #NERRU, AS A BIRD 120
THE DEATH OF THE LIZARD. 121
THE CAT'S SONG... 123
THE SONG OF THE CAAMA FOX. 125
THE SONGS OF THE BLUE CRANE. 126
THE OLD WOMAN'S SONG. 128
A SONG SUNG BY THE STAR !GAUNU, AND
    ESPECIALLY BY BUSHMAN WOMEN..................... 129
SIRIUS AND CANOPUS. 130
THE SONG OF THE BUSTARD... 131
THE SONG OF THE SPRINGBOK MOTHERS............. 132
||KABBO'S SONG ON THE LOSS OF HIS
    TOBACCO POUCH. 133
THE BROKEN STRING... 134
THE SONG OF !NU!NUMMA-!KWITEN. 135

B. HISTORY (NATURAL AND PERSONAL).

THE LEOPARD AND THE JACKAL. 139
DOINGS OF THE SPRINGBOK. 140
HABITS OF THE BAT AND THE PORCUPINE. 141
THE SAXICOLA CASTOR AND THE WILD CAT. 144
THE BABOONS AND ||XABBITEN||XABBITEN. 145
A LION'S STORY. 147
THE MAN WHO FOUND A LION IN A CAVE. 148
CERTAIN HUNTING OBSERVANCES, CALLED
    !NANNA-SSE. 151
!NANNA-SSE SECOND PART. 153
FURTHER INFORMATION; PARTICULARLY WITH
    REGARD TO THE TREATMENT OF BONES. 153
TREATMENT OF BONES BY THE NARRATOR'S
    GRANDFATHER, TSATSI. 157
HOW THE FATHER-IN-LAW OF THE
    NARRATOR TREATED BONES. 158
TACTICS IN SPRINGBOK HUNTING. 159
||KABBO'S CAPTURE AND JOURNEY TO CAPE
    TOWN. FIRST ACCOUNT. 160
||KABBO'S CAPTURE AND JOURNEY TO CAPE
    TOWN. SECOND ACCOUNT. 162
||KABBO'S JOURNEY IN THE RAILWAY TRAIN. 164
||KABBO'S INTENDED RETURN HOME. 165
HOW |HANG#KASS'O'S PET LEVERET
    WAS KILLED. 172
THE THUNDERSTORM. 174
CUTTING OFF THE TOP OF THE LITTLE FINGER,
    AND PIERCING EARS AND NOSE. 176
CUTTING OFF THE TOP OF THE LITTLE
    FINGER. SECOND ACCOUNT. 177
BUSHMAN PRESENTIMENTS 178
DOINGS AND PRAYERS WHEN CANOPUS
    AND SIRIUS COME OUT. 182
THE MAKING OF CLAY POTS. 184

THE BUSHMAN SOUP SPOON.	187
THE SHAPED RIB BONE.	188
THE BUSHMAN DRUM AND DANCING RATTLES.	189
HOW THE DANCING RATTLES ARE PREPARED.	190
THE USE OF THE !GOING!GOING, FOLLOWED BY AN ACCOUNT OF A BUSHMAN DANCE.	191
PREPARATION OF THE FEATHER BRUSHES USED IN SPRINGBOK HUNTING.	194
THE MARKING OF ARROWS.	196
THE ADHESIVE SUBSTANCE USED BY THE BUSHMEN IN MARKING ARROWS.	197
MODE OF GETTING RID OF THE EVIL INFLUENCE OF BAD DREAMS.	198
CONCERNING TWO APPARITIONS.	199
THE JACKAL'S HEART NOT TO BE EATEN.	202
ǀǀHARA AND TTO.	204
HOW TTO IS OBTAINED.	206
SIGNS MADE BY BUSHMEN IN ORDER TO SHOW IN WHICH DIRECTION THEY HAVE GONE.	207
A BUSHMAN, BECOMING FAINT FROM THE SUN'S HEAT WHEN RETURNING HOME, THROWS EARTH INTO THE AIR, THAT THOSE AT HOME MAY SEE THE DUST AND COME TO HELP HIM.	209
DEATH.	211
THE RELATIONS OF WIND, MOON, AND CLOUD TO HUMAN BEINGS AFTER DEATH.	214

APPENDIX.
A. FEW !KUNG TEXTS.

1. ǀXUE AS !NAXANE	219
2. FURTHER CHANGES OF FORM.	220
3. ǀXUE AS A ǀǀGUI TREE AND AS A FLY.	221
4. ǀXUE AS WATER AND AS OTHER THINGS. IN HIS OWN FORM, HE RUBS FIRE AND DIES.	222

PRAYER TO THE YOUNG MOON. 225
THE TREATMENT OF THIEVES. 226
THE FOUR PIECES OF WOOD CALLED |XU,
    USED FOR DIVINING PURPOSES. 229
TO BEAT THE GROUND (WITH A STONE) 231
SNAKES, LIZARDS, AND A CERTAIN SMALL
    ANTELOPE, WHEN SEEN NEAR GRAVES,
    TO BE RESPECTED. 232
A CERTAIN SNAKE, WHICH, BY LYING UPON
    ITS BACK, ANNOUNCES A DEATH IN THE
    FAMILY; AND WHICH MUST NOT, UNDER
    THESE CIRCUMSTANCES, BE KILLED. 233

PREFACE.

With all its shortcomings, after many and great difficulties, this volume of specimens of Bushman folk-lore is laid before the public. As will be seen from the lists given in Dr. Bleek's "Brief Account of Bushman Folk-lore and other Texts", Cape Town, 1875, and in my "Short Account of Further Bushman Material collected", London, 1889, the selections which have been made for it form but a very small portion of the Bushman native literature collected. Whether future days will see the remainder of the manuscripts, as well as the fine collection of copies of Bushman pictures made by the late Mr. G. W. Stow, also published is a question that only time can answer.

In the spelling of the native text in the volume now completed, various irregularities will be observed. These have their source chiefly in two causes. One of these was the endeavour always to write down, as nearly as possible, the sounds heard at the time; the other, that Dr. Bleek's orthography was of a more scientific kind than that of the other collector, whose ear had been mainly accustomed to English sounds.

In a few instances, the "new lines" in the native text and translation do not correspond; as the Bushman and English proofs had often to be sent over separately to Germany for correction.

The corresponding marginal numbers, by the side of the native texts and the translation (which refer to the pages in the original manuscripts), will, it is hoped, be of material assistance to those wishing to study the Bushman language from this volume.

With regard to the extra signs used in printing the Bushman texts, it should be explained that Dr. Block, in order to avoid still further confusion in the signs used to represent clicks, adopted the four marks for these which had already been employed by some of the missionaries in printing Hottentot. He added a horizontal line at the top of the mark |, used for the dental click, for the sake of additional clearness in writing (see the table of signs on page 438 of the Appendix). This addition he intended to discontinue when the time for printing should come; and it no longer appears in the table of signs he prepared for the printer in 1874. The sequence of the clicks, in this last table, he has also somewhat altered; and has substituted the mark ⓐ, instead of the previously used @ for the "gentle croaking sound in the throat".

| indicates the dental click.
! cerebral click.
|| lateral click.
palatal click.
ⓐ labial click.
X an aspirated guttural, like German ch.
Y a strong croaking sonud in the throat.
U a gentle croaking sound in the throat.
~ the nasal pronunciation of a syllable.
= under vowels, indicates a, rough, deep pronunciation of them.
indicates the raised tone.[1]
= indicates that the syllable under which it stands has a musical intonation.
` indicates an arrest of breath (as in *tt'uara*).

1. The tone is occasionally the only distinguishing feature in words spelt otherwise alike, but having a different meaning.

o placed under a letter, indicates a very short pronunciation of it.
—under a vowel, indicates a more or less open pronunciation of it.
ng indicates a ringing pronunciation of the n, as in "song" in English.
r placed over n indicates that the pronunciation is between that of the two consonants. There is also occasionally a consonantal sound met with in Bushman between r, n, and l.

A description of how to make the first four clicks, in this list, follows; taken from Dr. Bleek's "Comparative Grammar of South African Languages", Part I, Phonology, pp. 12 and 13.

The dental click | is sounded by pressing the "tip of the tongue against the front teeth of the upper jaw, and then suddenly and forcibly withdrawing it". (Tindall.) It resembles our interjection of annoyance.

The cerebral click ! is "sounded by curling up the tip of the tongue against the roof of the palate, and withdrawing it suddenly and forcibly" (Tindall.)

The lateral click || is, according to Tinddall, in Nama Hottentot generally articulated by covering with the tongue the whole of the palate, and producing the sound as far back as possible, either at what Lepsius calls the faucal or the guttaral point of the palate. European learners, however, imitate the sound by placing the tongue against the side teeth and then withdrawing it." * * * "A similar sound is often made use of in urging forward a horse."

The palatal click = is "sounded by pressing the tip of the tongue with as flat a surface as possible against the termination of the palate at the gums, and removing it in the same manner as during the articulation of the other clicks".

The labial click, marked by Dr. Bleek @, sounds like a kiss.

In the arrangement of these specimens of Bushman folk-lore, Dr. Bleek's division has been followed. The figures at the head of each piece refer to its number in one or other of the two Bushman Reports inentioned above. The letter B. or L. has been added, to show in which report it was originally included.

"The Resurrection of the Ostrich," and the parsing of a portion of it, were not finally prepared for the printer when Dr. Bleek died; and it was, here and there, very difficult to be sure of what had been his exact intention, especially in the parsing; but the papers were too important to be omitted.

The givers of the native literature in the "Specimens" are as follows:—

|*a!kungta* (who contributes two pieces) was a youth who came from a part of the country in or near the Strontbergen (lat. 30 deg S., long. 22 deg E.). He was with Dr. Bleek at Mowbray from August 29th, 1870, to October 15th, 1873.

||*kabbo* or "Dream" (who furnishes fifteen pieces) was from the same neighbourbood as |*a!kungta*. He was an excellent narrator, and patiently watched until a sentence had been written down, before proceeding with what he was telling. He much enjoyed the

17

thought that the Bushman stories would become known by means of books. He was with Dr. Bleek from February 16th, 1871, to October 15th,

1873. He intended to return, later, to help us at Mowbray, but, died before he could do so, |hang#kass'o or "Klein Jantje" (son-in-law to ||kabbo) contributes thirty-four pieces to this volume. He also was an excellent narrator; and remained with us from January 10th, 1878, to December, 1879.

Dia!kwain gives fifteen pieces, which are in the Katkop dialect, which Dr. Bleek found to vary slightly from that spoken by ||kabbo and |a!kungta. He came from the Katkop Mountains, north of Calvinia (about 200 miles to the west of the homes of |a!kungta and ||kabbo). He was at Mowbray from before Christmas, 1873, to March 18th, 1874, returning on June 13th, 1874, and remaining until March 7th, 1875.

!kweiten ta ||ken (a sister of Dia!kwain's) contributes three pieces, also in the Katkop dialect. She remained at Mowbray from June 13th, 1874, to January 13th, 1875.

|Xaken-ang, an old Bushman woman (fifth in a group of Bushman men and women, taken, at Salt River, in 1884), contributes one short fragment. She was with us, for a little while, in 1884; but, could not make herself happy at Mowbray. She longed to return to her own country, so that she might be buried with her forefathers.

To the pieces of native literature dictated by ||kabbo, no giver's name has been prefixed. To those supplied by the other native informants, their respective names have been added.

Portraits of ||kabbo, Dia!kwain, his sister, !kweiten ta ||ken, |hang#kass'o, and |Xaken-au will be seen among the illustrations; from which, by an unfortunate oversight, that of |a!kungta has been omitted.

The few texts in the language of the "Bushmen" calling themselves !kung, met with beyond Damaraland, which are given in the Appendix, are accompanied by as adequate an English translation as can at present be supplied. These texts were furnished by two lads, whose portraits will also be found among the illustrations. The extract given below, from the Bushman Report of 1889, sent in to the Cape Government, will explain a little more about them. The additional signs required for the printing of the !kung texts are almost similar to those employed in printing the Specimens of Bushman Folk-lore, but fewer in number.

"It had been greatly desired by Dr. Bleek to gain information regarding the language spoken by the Bushmen met with beyond Damaraland; and, through the most kind assistance of Mr. W. Coates Palgrave (to whom this wish was known), two boys of this race (called by itself !kung), from the country to the north-east of Damaraland, were, on the 1st of September, 1879, placed with us, for a time, at Mowbray. They were finally, according to promise, sent back to Damaraland, on their way to their own country, under the kind care of Mr. Eriksson, on the 28th of March, 1882. From these lads, named respectively !nanni and *Tamme*, much valuable information was obtained. They were, while with us, joined, for a time, by permission of the authorities, on the 25th of March 1880 by two younger boys from the same region named |uma and *Da*. The latter was very young at the time of his arrival; and was believed by the elder boys to belong to a different tribe of !kung. |uma left us, for an employer found for him by Mr. George Stevens, on the 12th of December, 11 1881, and *Da* was replaced in Mr. Stevens' kind care on the 29th of March, 1884. The language spoken by these lads (the two elder of whom, coming from a distance of fifty miles or so apart, differed slightly, dialectically, from each other) proved unintelligible to |hang#kass'o, as was his to them. They looked upon the Bushmen of the Cape Colony as being another kind of !kung; and |hang#kass'o, before he left us, remarked upon the existence of a partial resemblance between the language of the Grass Bushmen, and that spoken by the !kung. As far as I could observe, the language spoken by these lads appears to contain four clicks only; the labial click, in use among the Bushmen of the Cape Colony, etc., being the one absent; and the lateral click being pronounced in a slightly different manner.[1] The degree of relationship between the language spoken by the !kung and that of the Bushmen of the Cape Colony (in which the main portion of our collections had been made) has still to be determined. The two elder lads were fortunately also able to furnish some specimens of their native traditionary lore; the chief figure in which appears to be a small personage, possessed of magic power, and able to assume almost any form; who, although differently named, bears a good deal of resemblance to the Mantis, in the mythology of the Bushmen. The

1. It will be observed that, in some instances, in the earliercollected !kung texts, given in the Appendix, the mark !! has been used to denote the lateral click, in words where this differed slightly in its pronunciation from the ordinary lateral click, ||. Later, this attempt to distinguish these two sounds apart was discontinued.

power of imitating sounds, both familiar and unfamiliar to them, as well as the actions of animals, possessed by these boys, was astonishing. They also showed a certain power of representation, by brush and pencil. The arrows made by them were differently feathered, and more elaborately so than those in common use among the Bushmen of the Cape Colony."[1]

As the suggestion has been advanced that the painters and sculptors were from different divisions of the Bushman race, the following facts will be, of interest. One evening, at Mowbray, in 1875, Dr. Bleek asked *Dia!kwain* if he could make pictures. The latter smiled and looked pleased; but what he said has been forgotten. The following morning, early, as Dr. Bleek passed through the back porch of his house on his way to Cape Town, he perceived a small drawing, representing a family of ostriches, pinned to the porch wall, as *Dia!kwain* reply to his question. (See illustration thirty-three.) The same Bushman also told me, on a later occasion, that his father, *Xua-tting*, had himself chipped pictures of gemsbok, quaggas, ostriches, etc., at a place named *!kann* where these animals used to drink before the coming of the Boers. Some other drawings made by *Dia!kwain*, as well as a few by |*hang#kass'o*, and the *!kung* boys, will be found among the illustrations. In the arrangement of these, it has not, been easy to place them appropriately as regards

1. Taken from "A Short Account of further Bushman Material" collected By L. C. Lloyd.—Third Report concerning Bushman Researches, presented to both Houses of the Parliament of the Cape of Good Hope, ".—London: David Nutt, 270, Strand.—1889. pp. 4 & 5.

the text, as anything standing between text and translation would materially hinder the usefulness of the latter; and, for this reason, the main portion of the illustrations will be placed at the end of the volume.

To show the living activity of Bushman beliefs, the following instances may be given. Some little time after Dr. Bleek's death, a child, who slept in a small room by herself, had been startled by an owl making a sound, like breathing, outside her window in the night. This was mentioned to *Dia!kwain*, who said, with a much-pleased expression of countenance, did I not think that Dr. Bleek would come to see how his little children were getting on?

Later, I brought a splendid red fungus home from a wood in the neighbourhood of the Camp Ground, in order to ascertain its native name. After several days, fearing lest it should decay, I asked |*hang#kass'o*, who was then with us, to throw it away. Shortly afterwards, some unusually violent storms of wind and rain occurred. Something was said to him about the weather; and |*hang#kass'o* asked me If I did not remember telling him to throw the fungus away. He said, he had not done so, but had "put it gently down". He explained that the fungus was "a rain's thing"; and evidently ascribed the very bad weather, we were then having, to my having told him to "throw it away".

To Dr. Theal, for his most kind interest in this work, and for his untiring help with regard to its publication, to Professor von Luschan, for his kind efforts to promote the publication of the copies of Bushman pictures made by the late Mr. G. W. Stow, to *Herrn Regierungsbaumeister a.d.*, H. Werdelmann, for the copies of Bushman implements that he was so good as to make for us, to my niece, Doris Bleek, for her invaluable help in copying many of the manuscripts and making the Index to this volume, and to my niece, Edith Bleek, for much kind, assistance, my most grateful thanks are due.

L. C. LLOYD.

CHARLOTTENBURG, GERMANY.

May, 1911.

INTRODUCTION.

THE Bushmen were members of a division of the human species that in all probability once occupied the whole, or nearly the whole, of the African continent. It would seem that they were either totally exterminated or partly exterminated and partly absorbed by more robust races pressing down from the north, except in a few secluded localities where they could manage to hold their own, and that as a distinct people they bad disappeared from nearly the whole of Northern and Central Africa before white men made their first appearance there. Schweinfurth, Junker, Stanley, Von Wissmann,[1] and other explorers and residents in the equatorial

---

1. The following volumes may be referred to:—

Schweinfurth, Dr. George: *The Heart of Africa, Three Years' Travels and Adventures in the Unexplored Regions of Central Africa, from 1868 to 1871.* Two crown octavo volumes, published in London (date not given).

Junkier, Dr. Wilhelm: *Travels in Africa during the Years 1875-1886.* Translated from the German by A. H. Keane, F.R.G.S. Three demy octavo volumes, published in London in 1890-2.

Stanley, Henry N1.: *In Darkest Africa or the Quest, Resuce, and Retreat of Emin, Governor of Equatoria.* Two demy octavo volumes, published in London in 1890.

von Wissinann, Hermann: *My Second Journey through Equatorial Africa from the Congo to the Zambesi in the Years 1886 and 1887.* Translated from the German by Minna J. A. Bergmann. A demy octavo volume, published in London in 1891.

Casati, Major Gaetano: *Ten Years in Equatoria and the Return with Emin Pasha.* Translated from the original Italian Manuscript by the Hon. Mrs. J. Randolph Clay assisted by Mr. I. Walter Savage Lauder. Two royal octavo volumes, published at London aud New York in 1891.

Burrows, Captain Guy: *The Land of the Pygmies.* A demy octavo volume, published in London in 1898.

---

regions, who have had intercourse with the pygmies still existing in the depths of the dark forest west of the Albert Nyanza, have given descriptions of these people which show almost beyond a doubt that they and the Bushmen of South Africa are one in race. All the physical characteristics are the same, if we allow for the full open eye of the northern pygmy being due to his living in forest gloom, and the sunken half-closed eye of the southern Bushman to his life being passed in the glare of an unclouded sun.

The average height of adult male Bushmen, as given by Fritsch and other observers from careful measurement, is 144.4 centimetres or 56-85 inches. Von Wissmann gives the height of some pygmies that he measured as from 140 to 145 centimetres, or about the same.

Schweinfurth's description not only of the bodily but of the mental characteristics of his pygmy would hold good for one of the southern stock, Junker's photographs might have been taken on the Orange river; and no one acquainted with Bushman can read the charming account of the imp Blasiyo, given by Mrs. R. B. Fisher in lier book *On the Borders of Pygmy Land*, without recognising the aborigine of South Africa. Whether he is blowing a great horn and capering under the dining-room window, or caning the big Bantu men in the class which he is teaching to read in the mission school at Kabarole, in order to make them respect him, the portrait in words which Mrs. Fisher has given of that exceedingly interesting pygmy is true to the life of one of those with whom this volume deals.

But those isolated remnants of a race that there is every reason to believe was once widely spread do not offer to ethnologists such an excellent subject for study as might at first thought be supposed, for it would appear from the observations of travellers that they have lost their original language, though this is not altogether certain. Savages though having the passions and the bodily strength of men, are children in mind and children in the facility with which they acquire other forms of speech than those of their parents. The rapidity with which a Bushman learned to speak Dutch or English, when he was brought into contact with white people in South Africa, was regarded as almost marvellous in the early days of the Cape Colony. And so the Bushmen or pygmies of the north, hemmed in by Bantu, although not on friendly terms with them, learned to speak Bantu dialects and may have lost their own ancient tongue. This is to be gathered from what travellers have related, but no one has yet lived long enough with them to be able to say definitely that among themselves they do not speak a distinct language, and use a corrupt Bantu dialect when conversing with strangers. But whether this be so or not, they must have lost much of their original lore, or it must at least have changed its form.

South of the Zambesi and Kunene rivers, in addition to the Bushmen, two races had penetrated before our own. One of those was composed of the people termed by us Hottentots, who at a very remote time probably had Bushmen as one of its ancestral stocks, and certainly in recent centuries had incorporated great numbers of Bushman girls. But these people never went far from the coast, though they continued their migrations along the border of the ocean all the way round from the Kunene to a little beyond the Umzimvubu, where their further progress was stopped by the Bantu advancing on that side. Where they originally resided cannot be stated positively, but there is strong reason for believing that in ancient times they occupied the territory now called Somaliland. The references to Punt in early Egyptian history, and the portrait of the queen of that country so often described by different writers, may be mentioned as one of the indications leading to this belief. Another, and perhaps stronger, indication is the large number of drilled stones of the exact size and pattern of those used by the Hottentots in South Africa—different in form from those manufactured by Bushmen—that have been found in Somaliland, an excellent collection of which can, be seen in the ethnological museum in Berlin. The Hottentots, according to their own traditions, came from some far distant country in the northeast, and they cannot have crossed the Kunene many centuries before Europeans made their first appearance at the extremity of the continent. This is conclusively proved by the fact that the dialects spoken by the tribes in Namaqualand and beyond Algoa Bay on the south-eastern coast differed slightly that the people of one could understand the people of the other without much difficulty, which would certainly not have been the case if they had been many centuries separated. They had no intercourse with each other, and yet towards the close of the seventeenth century an interpreter belonging to a tribe in the neighbourbood of the Cape peninsula, when accompanying Dutch trading parties, conversed with ease with them all.

In our present state of knowledge it is impossible to say when the Bantu first crossed the Zambesi, because it is altogether uncertain whether there were, or were not, tribes of black men in the territory now termed Rhodesia before the ancestors of the present occupants moved down from the north; but those at present in the country cannot claim a possession of more than seven or eight hundred years. When the Europeans formed their first settlements, the area occupied by the Bantu was small compared with what it is today, and a vast region inland from the Kathlamba mountains nearly to the Atlantic shore was inhabited exclusively by Bushmen. That region included the whole of the present Cape province except the coast belt, the whole of Basutoland and the Orange Free State, the greater part, if not the whole, of the Transvaal province, and much of Betshuanaland, the Kalahari, and Hereroland. The paintings on rocks found in Southern Rhodesia at the present day afford proof of a not very remote occupation by Bushmen of that territory, but they give evidence also that the big dark-coloured Bantu were already there as well.

By the Hottentots and the Bantu the Bushmen were regarded simply as noxious animals, and though young girls were usually spared and incorporated in the tribes of their captors to lead a life of drudgery and shame, all others who could be entrapped or hunted down were destroyed with as little mercy as if they had been hyenas. On the immediate border of the Hottentot and Bantu settlements there was thus constant strife with the ancient race, but away from that frontier line the Bushmen pursued their game and drank the waters that their fathers had drunk from time immemorial, without even the knowledge that men differing from themselves existed in the world.

This was the condition of things when in the year 1652 the Dutch East India Company formed a station for refreshing the crews of its fleets on the shore of Table Bay, a station that has grown into the present British South Africa. The Portuguese had established themselves at Sofala a hundred and forty-seven years earlier, but they had never penetrated the country beyond the Bantu belt, and consequently never made the acquaintance of Bushmen. From 1652 onward there was an opportunity for a thorough study of the mode of living, the power of thought, the form of speech, the religious ideas, and all else that can be known of one of the most interesting savage races of the earth, a race that there is good reason to believe once extended not only over Africa, but over a large part of Europe, over South-Eastern Asia, where many scientists maintain it is now represented by the Semang in the Malay peninsula, the Andamanese, and some of the natives of the Philippine islands,-and possibly over a much greater portion of the world's surface, a race that had made little, if any, advance since the far distant days when members of it shot their flint-headed arrows at reindeer in France, and carved the figures of mammoths and other now extinct animals on tusks of ivory in the same fair land. It was truly an ancient race, one of the most primitive that time had left on the face of the earth.

But there were no ethnologists among the early white settlers, whose sole object was to earn their bread and make homes for themselves in the new country where their lot was cast. They too soon came to regard the wild Bushmen as the Hottentots and the Bantu regarded them, as beings without a right to the soil over which they roamed, as untamable robbers whom it was not only their interest but their duty to destroy. They took possession of the fountains wherever they chose, shot the game that the pygmies depended upon for food, and when these retaliated by driving off oxen and sheep, made open war upon the so-called marauders. It was impossible for pastoral white men and savage Bushmen who neither cultivated the ground nor owned domestic cattle of any kind to live side by side in amity and peace. And so, slowly but surely, the Europeans, whether Dutch or English, extended their possessions inland, the Hottentots-Koranas and Griquas,-abandoning the coast, made their way also into the interior, and the Bantu spread themselves ever farther and farther, until today there is not an acre of land in all South Africa left to the ancient race. Every man's hand was against them, and so they passed out of sight, but perished fighting stubbornly, disdaining compromise or quarter to the very last. There is no longer room on the globe for palæolithic man.

When I say every man's hand was against them, I do not mean to imply that no efforts at all were ever made by white men to save them from absolute extinction, or that no European cast an eye of pity upon the unfortunate wanderers. On more than one occasion about the beginning of the nineteenth century benevolent frontier farmers collected horned cattle, sheep, and goats, and endeavoured to induce parties of Bushmen to adopt a pastoral life, but always without success. They could not change their habits suddenly, and so the stock presented to them was soon consumed. The London

Missionary Society stationed teachers at different points among them, but could not prevail upon them to remain at any one place longer than they were supplied with food. In the middle of the same century the government of the Orange River Sovereignty set apart reserves for two little bands of them, but by some blunder located a Korana clan between them, and that effort failed. Then many frontier farmers engaged families of Bushmen to tend their flocks and herds, which they did as a rule with the greatest fidelity until they became weary of such a monotonous life, and then they wandered away again. Other instances might be added, but they all ended in the same manner. The advance of the white man, as well as of the Hottentots and the Bantu, was unavoidably accompanied with the disappearance of the wild people.

On the farms where a number of Bushman families lived white children often learned to speak their language, with all its clicks, and smacking of the lips, and guttural sounds, but this knowledge was of no use to anyone but themselves, and it died with them. They were incompetent to reduce it to writing and too ill-educated to realise the value of the information they possessed. Here and there a traveller of scientific attainments, such as Dr. H. Lichtenstein, or a missionary of talent, such as the reverend T. Arbousset, tried to form a vocabulary of Bushman words, but as they did not understand the language theinselves, and there were no recognised symbols to represent the various sounds, their lists are almost worthless to philologists.

So matters stood in 1857, when the late Dr. Wilhelm H. I. Bleek (Ph.D.), who was born at Berlin in 1827, and educated at the universities of Bonn and Berlin, commenced his researches in connection with the Bushmen. He was eminently qualified for the task, as his natural bent was in the direction of philology, and his training had been of the very best kind, in that he had learned from it not to cease study upon obtaining his degree, but to continue educating himself. For many years after 1857, however, he did not devote himself entirely, or even mainly, to investigations regarding the Bushmen, because of the difficulty of obtaining material, and also because he was intently engaged upon the work with which his reputation as a philologist inust ever be connected, *A Comparative Granmar of South African Languages*. In this book he deals with the Hottentot language and with the Bantu, the last divided into a large number of dialects. In 1862 the first part of his valuable work appeared, in 1864 a small volume followed entitled *Renyard the Fox in South Africa, or Hottentot Fables and Tales*, and in 1869 the first section of the second part of his *Comparative Grammar* was published. That work, regarded by everyone since its issue as of the highest value, and which must always remain the standard authority on its subject, was never completed, for in 1870 a favourable opportunity of studying the Bushman language occurred, of which Dr. Bleek at once availed himself, knowing that in the few wild people left he had before him the fast dying remnant of a primitive race, and that if any reliable record of that race was to be preserved, not a day must be lost in securing it.

To abandon a work in which fame had been gained, which offered still further celebrity in its prosecution, and to devote himself entirely to a new object, simply because the one could be completed by somebody else at a future time, and the other, if neglected then, could never be done at all, shows such utter devotion to science, such entire forgetfulness of self, that the name of Dr. Bleek should be uttered not only with the deepest respect, but with a feeling akin to reverence. How many men of science are there in the world today who would follow so noble an example?

The task now before him was by no means a simple or an easy one. The few pure Bushmen that remained alive were scattered in the wildest and most inaccessible parts of the country, and it would have been useless to search for them there. A traveller indeed, who was prepared to live in a very rough manner himself, might have found a few of them, but his intercourse with them would necessarily have been so short that he could not study thenithoroughly. But, fortunately for science, unfortunately for the wretched creatures themselves, the majesty of European law had brought several of them within reach. That law, by a proclamation of the earl of Caledon, governor of the Cape Colony, issued on the 1st of November 1809, had confounded them with the Hottentots, and made all of them within the recognised boundaries British subjects, but had placed them under certain restraints, which were intended to prevent them from roaming about at will. It had very little effect upon the wild people, however, who were almost as difficult to arrest on the thinly occupied border as if they had been baboons. Then, in April 1812, by a proclamation of Governor

Sir John Cradock, their children, when eight years of age, if they had lived on a farm since their buth, were apprenticed by the local magistrate for ten years longer. In this proclamation also they were confounded with Hottentots, and it really had a considerable effect upon them, because it was no uncommon circumstance for Bushman parents to leave their infant children on farms where they had been in service, and not return perhaps for a couple of years.

By a colonial ordinance of the 17th of July 1828 all restraints of every kind were removed from these people, and they had thereafter exactly the same amount of freedom and of political rights as Europeans. It seems absurd to speak of Bushmen having political rights, for their ideas of government were so crude that their chiefs were merely leaders in war and the chase, and had no judicial powers, each individual liaving the right to avenge his own wrongs; but so, the law determined. It determined also that the ground upon which their ancestors for ages had hunted should be parcelled out in farms and allotted to European settlers, and that if they went there afterwards and killed or drove away an ox or a score of sheep, they could be sentenced to penal servitude for several years. It seems hard on the face of it, but progress is remorseless, and there was no other way of extending civilisation inland. The pygmy hunter with his bow and poisoned arrows could not be permitted to block the way.

But he, though he could not argue the matter, and regarded it as the most natural thing in the world for the strong to despoil the weak, being the feeble one himself resented this treatment. He was hungry too, terribly hungry, for the means of sustenance in the arid wastes where be was making his last stand were of the scantiest, and he longed for meat, such meat as his fathers had eaten before the Hottentots and the big black men and the white farmers came into the country and slaughtered all the game and nearly all of his kin. And so he tightened his hunger belt, and crept stealthily to a hill-top, where he could make observations without anyone noticing him, and when night fell he stole down to the farmer's fold and before day dawned again he and his companions were gorged with flesh. When the farmer arose and discovered his loss there was a big hunt as a matter of course. Man and horse and dog were pressed into the chase, and yet so wily was the little imp, so expert in taking cover, and it must be added so feared were his poisoned arrows, that it was a rare thing for him to be captured. Once in a while, however, he was made a prisoner, and then if it could be proved that he had killed a shepherd he was hanged, but if he could be convicted of nothing more than slaughtering other men's oxen and sheep he was sent to a convict station for a few years.

So it came about that Dr. Bleek found at the convict station close to Capetown several of the men he wanted. There were two in particular, whose terms of imprisonment bad nearly expired, and who were physically unfit for hard labour. The government permitted him to take these men to his own residence, on condition of locking them up at night until the remainder of their sentences expired. After they had returned to the place of their birth, two other Bushmen were obtained, who ere long were induced to proceed to their old haunts and prevail upon some of their relatives to accompany them back again, so that at one time a whole family could be seen on Dr. Bleck's grounds.

The material was thus obtained to work with, but first the language of the primitive people had to be learned, a language containing so many clicks and other strange sounds that at first it seemed almost impossible for all adult European tongue to master it. To this task Dr. Bleek and his sister-in-law Miss Lucy C. Lloyd, who had boundless patience, untiring zeal, and a particularly acute ear, devoted themselves, and persevered until their efforts were crowned with success. Symbols were adopted to represent the different sounds that are foreign to the European ear, and then it became possible to take down the exact words used by the Bushman narrators and to have the manuscript checked by repetition.

Before the results of such prolonged labour were ready for publication, but not until a very large quantity of valuable matter had been collected, to the great loss of students of man everywhere Dr. Bleek died, 17th of August 1875, Miss Lloyd then continued during some years to collect further material frorn. various individuals of the Bushman race, and after adding greatly to the stock on hand at her brother-in-law's death in 1887 she proceeded to Europe with a view to arranging it properly and ptiblishing it. For nine years she endeavoured, but in vain to carry out this design, the subject not being considered by publishers one that would attract readers in sufficient number to repay the cost of printing, as that cost would necessarily be large, owing to the style of the Bushman text. In

1896 Messrs. Swan Sonnenschein & Co. undertook to get out a volume, but then, unfortunately, Miss Lloyd fell ill, and her impaired strength has since that time delayed the completion of the work. It has only been at long intervals and by dint of much exertion that what is here presented to the reader, with much more that may perhaps follow, has been got ready. This is a brief account of the manner in which the material was collected, and of the causes which have delayed its publication for so many years. It would be quite impossible to gather such information now.

As to the value for scientific purposes (if the contents of this volume, a great deal might be stated, but it cannot be necessary to say much here, as the book speaks for itself. The religion of the Bushmen is made as clear from their own recitals as such a subject can be, when it is remembered that the minds of the narrators were like those of little children in all matters not connected with their immediate bodily wants. Their views concerning the sun, moon, and stars seem utterly absurd, but a European child five or six years of age, if not informed, would probably give no better explanation. Their faith too, that is, their unreasoning belief in many things adult European seem ridiculous, is seen to be that of mere infants. Every reader of this book has gone through the same stage of thought and mental power him or herself, and our own far remote ancestors must have had beliefs similar to those of Bushmen. The civilised European at different stages of his existence is a representative of the whole human species in its progress upward from the lowest savagery. We may therefore pity the ignorant pygmy, but we are not justified in despising him.

On many of their customs a flood of light is thrown in this volume, but I shall only refer to one here. In the early Dutch records of the Cape Colony there is an account of some Bushmen eating almost the whole of an animal, the intestines included, rejecting only two little pieces of flesh containing the sinews of the thighs. When questioned concerning this, they merely replied that it was their custom. not to eat those parts, beyond which no information is given. Who could have imagined the cause of such a custom? They had devoured parts tougher to masticate, so it certainly was not to spare their teeth. That is all that could be said of it, but here in this volume the reason is given, and how well it fits in with the belief of the wild people that certain men and animals could exchange their forms, that some animals in former times were men, and some men in former times were animals.

Probably, however, the value of this volume will be greatest to the philologist, as the original Bushman text, which will be unintelligible to the general reader, is printed side by side with the English translation. Students of the growth of language have thus the means of ascertaining how ideas were expressed by a race of people so low in culture as the Bushmen. Their vocabulary, it will be seen, was ample for their needs. What is surprising is that, though they had no word for a numeral higher than three, and though the plurals of many of their nouns were formed in such a simple manner as by reduplication, their verbs were almost, if not quite, as complete and expressive as our own. The myths indicate a people in the condition of early childhood, but from the language it is evident that in the great chain of human life on this earth the pygmy savages represented a link much closer to the modern European end than to that of the first beings worthy of the name of men.

GEO. McCALL THEAL.

LONDON, 1911.

Think they are studying an early phase of human evolution.

A. MYTHOLOGY, FABLES, LEGENDS, AND POETRY

I. THE MANTIS.

THE MANTIS ASSUMES THE FORM OF A HARTEBEEST.

The Mantis is one who cheated the children, by becoming a hartebeest, by resembling a dead-hartebeest. He feigning death lay in front of the children, when the children went to seek gambroo (|kui, a sort of cucumber); because he thought (wished) that the children should cut him up with a stone knife, as these children did not possess metal knives.

The children perceived him, when he had laid himself stretched out, while his horns were turned backwards. The children then said to each other: "It is a hartebeest that yonder lies; it is dead." The children jumped for joy (saying): "Our hartebeest! we shall eat great meat." They broke off stone knives by striking (one stone against another), they skinned the Mantis. The skin of the Mantis snatched itself quickly out of the children's hands. They say to each other: "Hold thou strongly fast for me the hartebeest skin!" Another child said: "The hartebeest skin pulled at me."

Her elder sister said: "It does seem that the hartebeest has not a wound from the people who shot it; for, the hartebeest appears to have died of itself. Although the hartebeest is fat, (yet) the hartebeest has no shooting wound."

Her elder sister cut off a shoulder of the hartebeest, and put it down (on a bush). The hartebeest's shoulder arose by itself, it sat down nicely (on the other side of the bush), while it placed itself nicely. She (then) cut off a thigh of the hartebeest, and put it down (on a bush); it placed itself nicely on the bush. She cut off another shoulder of the hartebeest, and put it upon (another) bush.

It arose, and sat upon a soft (portion of the) bush; as it felt that the bush (upon which the child had laid it) pricked it.

Another elder sister cut off the other thigh of the hartebeest. They spoke thus: "This hartebeest's flesh does move;[1] that must be why it shrinks away."

They arrange their burdens; one says to the other: "Cut and break off the hartebeest's neck, so that (thy) younger sister may carry the hartebeest's head, for, (thy) yonder sitting elder sister, she shall carry the hartebeest's back, she who is a big girl. For, we must carrying return (home); for, we came (and) cut up this hartebeest. Its flesh moves;

---

1. The children truly thought that the hartebeest's flesh moved. The hartebeest's flesh seemed as if it was not hartebeest; for, the hartebeest's flesh was like a man's flesh, it moved.

   (As regards) a man's flesh, when another man shoots him, the poison enters the body. The people cutting break away his flesh, while they cutting take away the mouth of the poisonous wound. The people set aside the man's flesh; it remains quivering, while the other part of the flesh moves (quivers) in his body,-that (flesh) which he sits in (literally "which he possesses sitting"),that which the people cutting broke. This it is which moves in the (cut out) wound's mouth, while the flesh feels that the flesh is warm. Therefore, the flesh moves, as (while) the flesh (feels that the flesh) is alive; hence it is warm. As (while) the man (feels that he) warms himself at the fire, all his flesh is warm, while it (feels that it) lives. The thing (reason) on account of which he really dies is that his flesh feels cool. While it feels that it is cold, his flesh becomes very cold. This is the reason why his flesh dies.

---

its flesh snatches itself out of our hand. |*atta!*| it of itself places itself nicely."

They take up the flesh of the Mantis; they say to the child: "Carry the hartebeest's head, that father may put it to roast for you." The child slung on the hartebeest's head, she called to her sisters "Taking hold help me up;[2] this hartebeest's head is not light." Her sisters taking hold of her help her up.

They go away, they return (home). The hartebeest's head slips downwards, because the Mantis's head wishes to stand on the ground. The child lifts it up (with her shoulders), the hartebeest's head (by turning a little) removes the thong from the hartebeest's eye. The hartebeest's head was whispering, it whispering said to the child: "O child! the thong is standing in front of my eye. Take away for me the thong; the thong is shutting my eye." The child looked behind her; the Mantis winked at the child. The child whimpered;

her elder sister looked back at her. Her elder sister called to her: "Come forward quickly; we return (home)."

The child exclaimed: "This hartebeest's head is able to speak." Her elder sister scolded her: "Lying come forward; we go. Art thou not coming deceiving (us) about the hartebeest's head?"

The child said to her elder sister: "The hartebeest has winked at me with the hartebeest's eye; the hartebeest desired that I should take away the thong

1. This seems to be an exclamation, the meaning of which is not yet known to the editor.
2. The child lay upon her back upon the hartebeest's head.

from his eye. Thus it was that the hartebeest's head lay looking behind my back."

The child looked back at the hartebeest's head, the hartebeest opened and shut its eyes. The child said to her elder sister: "The hartebeest's head must be alive, for it is opening and shutting its eyes."

The child, walking on, unloosened the thong; the child let fall the hartebeest's head. The Mantis scolded the child, he complained about his head. He scolded the child: "Oh! oh! my head!¹ Oh! bad little person!² hurting me in my head."

Her sisters let fall the flesh of the Mantis. The flesh of the Mantis sprang together, it quickly joined itself to the lower part of the Mantis's back. The head of the Mantis quickly joined (itself) upon the top of the neck of the Mantis. The neck of the Mantis quickly joined (itself) upon the upper part of the Mantis's spine. The upper part of the Mantis's spine joined itself to the Mantis's back. The thigh of the Mantis sprang forward,³ it joined itself to the Mantis's back. His other thigh ran forward, racing it joined itself to the other side of the Mantis's back. The chest of the Mantis ran forward, it joined itself to the front side of the upper part of the Mantis's spine. The shoulder blade of the Mantis ran forward, it joined itself on to the ribs of the Mantis.

1. He was merely complaining about his head.
2. Mantis pronunciation of |nu!kui@ua wwe. The cursing of the Flat Bushmen. When a Flat Bushman is angry with another, then it is that he is wont to say |nu!kui, resembling |nussale (the name by which the Flat Bushmen call the Grass Bushmen),

for the other one's name. When he loves another person he is wont to say 'mate'; lie is wont to say 'brother' when they love each other.
3. The Mantis's thigh sprang forward like a frog.

The other shoulder blade of the Mantis ran forward, while it felt that the ribs of the Mantis had joined themselves on, when they raced.

The children still ran on; he (the Mantis, arose from the ground and) ran, while be chased the children,—he being whole,—his head being round, while he felt that he was a man.[1] Therefore, he was stepping along with (his) shoes, while he jogged with his shoulder blade.[2]

He saw that the children had reached home; he quickly turned about, be, jogging with his shoulder blade, descended to the river. He went along the river bed, making a noise as he stepped in the soft sand; he yonder went quickly out of the river bed. He returned, coming out at a different side of the house (ie. his own house) he returned, passing in front of the house.

The children said: "We have been (and) seen a hartebeest which was dead. That hartebeest, it was the one which we cut up with stone knives; its flesh quivered. The hartebeest's flesh quickly snatched itself out of our hands. It by itself was placing itself nicely upon bushes which were comfortable; while the hartebeest felt that the hartebeest's head would go along whispering. While the child who sits (there) carried it, it talking stood behind the child's back."

The child said to her father "O papa! Dost thou seem to think that the hartebeest's head did not talk to me? For the hartebeest's head felt that it would be looking at my hole above the nape of the

1. He became a man while he was putting himself together again.
2. With his left shoulder blade, he being a left-handed man.

neck, as I went along; and then it was that the hartebeest's head told me that I should take away for him the thong from his eye. For, the thong lay in front of his eye."

Her father said to them: "Have you been and cut up the old man, the Mantis, while he lay pretending to be dead in front of you?"

The children said: "We thought that the hartebeest's horns were there, the hartebeest had hair. The hartebeest was one which had not an arrow's wound; while the hartebeest felt that the hartebeest would talk. Therefore, the hartebeest came and chased us, when we bad put down the hartebeest's flesh. The hartebeest's flesh jumped together, while it springing gathered (itself) together, that it might mend, that it might mending hold together to the hartebeest's back. The hartebeest's back also joined on.

"Therefore, the hartebeest ran forward, while his body was red, when he had no hair (that coat of hair in which he had been lying down), as he ran, swinging his arm like a man.

"And when he saw that we reached the house, he whisked round, He ran, kicking up his heels (showing the white soles of his shoes), while running went before the wind, while the sun shone upon his feet's face (soles), while he ran with-all his might into the little river (bed), that he might pass behind the back of the hill lying yonder."

Their parents said to the children: "You are those who went and cut up the old man 'Tinderbox Owner.' He, there behind, was one who gently came out from the place there behind."

The children said to their fathers: "He has gone round, he ran fast. He always seems as if he would come over the little hill lying yonder when he sees that we are just reaching home. While this little daughter, she was the one to whom the hartebeest's head, going along, talked; and then she told us. Therefore, we let fall the hartebeest's flesh; we laid our karosses on our shoulders, that we might run very fast.

"While its flesh running came together on its back, it finished mending itself. He arose and ran forward, he, quickly moving his arms, chased us. Therefore, we did thus, we became tired from it, on account of the running with which he had chased us, whil e he did verily move his arms fast.

"Then he descended into the small river,-while he thought that he would, moving his arms fast, run along the small river. Then he thus did, he, picking up wood, came out; while we sat, feeling the fatigue; because he had been deceiving. While he felt that all the people saw him, when we came carrying his thighs, when he went to die lying in front of us; while he wished that we should feel this fatigue, while this child here, it carried his head,he looked up with fixed eyes. He was as if he was dead; he was (afterwards) opening and shutting his eyes; he afar lay talking (while the children were running off). He talked while be mended his body; his head talked, while he mended his body. His head talking reached his back; it came to join upon the top (of his neck).

"He ran forward; lie yonder will sit deceiving,(at home), while we did cut him up with stone knives (splinters). |*a-tta*! he went feigning death to lie in front of us, that we might do so, we run.

"This fatigue, it is that which we are feeling; and our hearts burnt on account of it. Therefore, we shall not hunt (for food), for we shall altogether remain at home."

!GAUNU-TSAXAU (THE SON OF THE MANTIS), THE BABOONS, AND THE MANTIS.

!gaunu-tsaxau [1] formerly went to fetch for his father sticks, that his father might take aim at the people who sit upon (their) heels. Fetching, he went up to them (the baboons) as they were going along feeding. Therefore, a baboon who feeding went past him,-he who was an older baboon,-he was the one to whom !gaunu-tsaxau came. Then he questioned !gaunu-tsaxau. And !gaunu-tsaxau told him about it, that he must fetch for his father sticks, that his father might take aim at the people who sit upon (their) heels. Therefore, he (the baboon) exclaimed [2] "Hie! Come to listen to this child." And the other one said:

> "First going
> I listen,
> To the child yonder.
> First going
> I listen,
> To the child yonder."

1 !gaunu-tsaxau was a son of the Mantis.
2. I must (the narrator here explained) speak in my language, because I feel that the speech of the baboons is not easy."

And he reached them. He said: "What does this child say?" And the child said: "I must fetch for my father sticks (bushes?), that my father may take aim at the people who sit upon (their) heels." Then the baboon said: "Tell the old man yonder that he must come to hear this child." Then the baboon called out: "Hie! Come to hear this child." Then the other one said:

> First going
> I listen,
> To the child yonder."

And he came up (to them); he exclaimed: "What does this child say? "And the other one answered: "This child, he wishes, he says, to fetch sticks for his father, that his father may take aim at the people who sit upon (their) heels." And this baboon said: "Tell the old man yonder that he must come to hear this child." Then this (other) baboon called out: "O person passing across in front! come to listen to this child." Therefore, the other one said:

> First going
> I listen,
> To the child yonder."

And he came up (to them). He said: "What does this child say?" And the other one answered: "This child wants, he says, to fetch sticks [1] for his father, that his father may take aim at the people who sit upon (their) heels." Therefore, this baboon

---

1. In a paper entitled "A Glimpse into the Mythology of the Maluti Bushmen," which appeared in the *Cape Monthly Magazine* for July, 1874, written by Mr. J. M. Orpen. (at that time Chief Magistrate, St. John's Territory), we find, on p. 8, that the Mantis sent one of his sons to cut sticks to make bows, and that he was caught and killed by the baboons.

---

exclaimed It is ourselves! Thou shalt tell the old man yonder that he sball come to listen to this child." Therefore, this other baboon called out: "Ho! come to listen to this child." Then the other one said:

> First going
> I listen,
> To the child yonder."

He came up to the other people on account of it. He said: "What does this child say?" And the other one answered: "This child, he wants, he says, to fetch[1] sticks for his father, that his father may take aim at the people who sit upon (their) heels." Therefore, this baboon exclaimed (with a sneering kind of laugh): "O ho! It is ourselves! Thou shalt quickly go to tell the old man yonder, that he may come to listen to this child." And the other one called out: "O person passing across in front! come to listen to this child." And the other said:

> First going
> I listen,
> To the child yonder."

And he went up to the other people; he said: "What does this child say?" And the other one answered: "This child, he wants, he says, to fetch sticks for his father, that his father may take aim at the people who sit upon their heels."

Then that baboon,—he felt that he was an old

1. Note by the narrator. He had sent his son, that his son should go to construct things for him. I think that they were sticks (bushes?). He wished his son to go (and) make them for him, that he might come (and) work them, in order that he might make war upon the baboons.

baboon—therefore, he said, when the other one had said, "This child wanted, he said, to fetch sticks for his father," therefore the other one (the old baboon) exclaimed: "What? it is we ourselves; ourselves it is! Ye shall strike the child with your fists."

Therefore, they were striking *!gaunu-tsaxau* with their fists on account of it; they hit with their fists, breaking (his) head. And another struck with his fist, knocking out *!gaunu-tsaxau*'s eye, the and the child's eye in this manner sprang (or rolled) away. Then this baboon exclaimed: "My ball! my ball! "Therefore, they began to play a game at ball,[2] while the child died; the child lay still. They said (sang):

> And I want it,
> Whose ball is it?
> And I want it,
> Whose ball is it?
> And I want it."

The other people said:

> My companion's ball it is,
> And I want it,
> My companion's ball it is,
> And I want it,"

while they were playing at ball there with the child's eye.

The Mantis was waiting for the child. Therefore, the Mantis lay down at noon. Therefore, the Mantis

1 (They) were playing at ball.

> My ball,
> My ball it is,
> And I want it.
> My companion's ball it is,
> And I want it,
> My companion's ball,
> And I want it."

was dreaming about the child, that the baboons were those who had killed the child; that they had made a ball of the child's eye; that he went to the baboons, while the baboons played at ball there with the child's eye.

Therefore, he arose; he took up the quiver, he slung on the quiver; be said, "Rattling along,[1] rattling along," while he felt that he used formerly to do so, he used to say, Rattling along." Then, when he came into sight. he perceived the baboons' dust, while the baboons were playing at ball there with the child's eye. Then the Mantis cried on account of it, because the baboons appeared really to have killed the child. Therefore, they were playing at ball there with the child's eye. Therefore, when he came into sight, he perceived the baboons' dust, while the baboons were playing at ball there with the child's eye. Therefore he cried about it. And he quickly shut his mouth; he thoroughly dried the tears from his eyes, while he desired that the baboons should not perceive tears in his eyes; that he appeared to have come crying, hence tears were in his eyes; so that he might go to play at ball with the baboons, while his eyes had no tears in them.

Then he, running, came up to the baboons, while the baboons stared at him, because they were startled at him.[2] Then, while the baboons were still staring at him, he came running to a place where he

1 The arrows they were, the arrows which were in the quiver; they made a rattling noise, because they stirred inside (it). Therefore, he said, "Rattling along, rattling along."
2. They were not in the habit of seeing him; therefore they stared at him.

laid down the quiver; he took off (his) kaross (i.e. skin cloak), he put down the kaross, he, grasping, drew out the feather brush which he had put into the bag, he shook out the brush, he played with (?) the ball. He called out to the baboons, why was it that the baboons were staring at him, while the baboons did not play with (?) the ball, that the baboons might throw it to him.

Then the baboons looked at one another, because they suspected why he spoke thus. Then he caught hold of the ball, when the ball had merely flown to another baboon, when this (the first) baboon had thrown the ball to the other. Then the child's eye, because the child's eye felt that it was startled (?), on account of his father's scent, it went playing about; the baboons trying to get it, missed it. Then one baboon, he was the one who caught hold of it, he threw it towards another. Then the Mantis merely sprang out from this place, the Mantis caught hold of the child's eye, the Mantis, snatching, took the child's eye. Then the Mantis whirled around the child's eye; he anointed the child's eye with (the perspiration of) his armpits. Then he threw the child's eye towards the baboons, the child's eye ascended, the child's eye went about in the sky; the baboons beheld it above, as it played about above in the sky. And the child's eye went to stand yonder opposite to the quiver; it appeared as if it sprang over the quiver, while it stood inside the quiver's bag.[1]

1. He tied, placing a little bag at the side of the quiver; therefore it is the quiver's bag; while it feels that it is a little bag which is tied at the side of the quiver; he had laid the bow upon it; it was the one that he tied, placing it by the side of the quiver. That bag, it was the one that the child's eye was in. That bag, it was the one that he laid the bow upon.

Then the baboons went to seek for it. The Mantis also sought for it, while the baboons sought for it. Then all the baboons were altogether seeking for the child's eye. They said: "Give my companion the ball."[1] The baboon whose ball it was, he said: "Give me the ball."[2] The Mantis said: "Behold ye! I have not got the ball." The baboons said: "Give my companion the ball." The baboon whose ball it was, he said: "Give me the ball." Then the baboons[3] said that the Mantis must shake the bag, for the ball seemed to be inside the bag. And the Mantis exclaimed: "Behold ye! Behold ye! the ball is not inside the bag. Behold ye!" while he grasped the child's eye, he shook, turning the bag inside out. He said: "Behold ye! Behold ye! the ball cannot be inside the bag."

Then this baboon exclaimed: "Hit the old man with (your) fists." Then the other one exclaimed: "Give my companion the ball! "while he struck the head of the Mantis. Then the Mantis exclaimed: "I have not got the ball," while he struck the baboon's head. Therefore, they were all striking the Mantis with their fists; the Mantis was striking them with his fist. Then the Mantis got the worst of it; the Mantis exclaimed: "Ow! Hartebeest's Children![4] ye must go! *!kau*

1. "Give my companion the ball."
2. "Give me the ball."
3. It is uncertain whether this should be singular or plural here.
4. "Hartebeest's Children," here, may refer to a bag made from the skin of young hartebeests, which the Mantis had with him.

!Yerriggu![1] ye must go!" while the baboons watched him ascend; as he flew up, as he flew to the water. Then he popped into the water on account of it; while he exclaimed: "*I | ke, tten !khwaiten!khwaiten, !kui ha i | ka!*"[2] "Then he walked out of the water; he sat down; he felt inside (his) bag; he took out the child's eye; he walked on as he held it; he walked, coming up to the grass at the top of the water's bank[3]; he sat down. He exclaimed: "*Oh wwi ho!*"[4] as he put the child's eye into the water.

"Thou must grow out, that thou mayest become like that which thou hast been."[5] "Then he walked on; he went to take up (his) kaross, he threw it over his shoulder; be took up the quiver, he slung on the quiver; and, in this manner, he returning went, while he returning arrived at home.

Then the young Ichneumon exclaimed: "Who can have done thus to my grandfather, the Mantis, that the Mantis is covered with wounds? "Then the Mantis replied: "The baboons were those who killed grandson, *!gaunu-tsaxau,* I went [the Mantis speaks very sadly and slowly here], as they were

1. The meaning of *!kau !Yerri-ggu* is at present unknown to the translator, but the Mantis is still addressing some of his possessions, and ordering them to leave the scene of his defeat.
2. Of these words of the Mantis (which frequently appear in stories concerning him) the narrators were not able to furnish a sufficiently clear explanation, so the original text is given.
3. It is grass; the grass which stands upon the top of the water's bank; it is that which the Bushmen call | *kannung-a-sse.*
4. At the same time, putting the first finger of his right hand into his mouth, against his left cheek, and drawing it forcibly out; the eye being meanwhile in the palm of his right hand, shut down by his other fingers.
5 He desired that the child should live; that it should living return.

playing at ball there with grandson's eye; I went to play at ball with them. Then grandson's eye vanished. Therefore, the baboons said (that) I was the one who had it; the baboons were fighting me; therefore, I was fighting them; and I thus did, I flying came."

Then | *kuammang-a* said: "I desire thee to say to grandfather, Why is it that grandfather continues to go among strangers [literally, people who are different]?" Then the Mantis answered: "Thou dost appear to think that yearning was not that on account of which I went among the baboons; "while he did not tell | *kuammang-a* and the others that he came (and) put the child's eye into the water.

Then he remained there (i.e. at home), while he did not go to the water. Then he went there, while he went to look at the place where he had put in the child's eye. And he approached gently, while he wished that he might not make a rustling noise. Therefore, he gently came. And the child heard him, because he had not come gently when afar off; and the child jumped up, it splashed into the water. Then the Mantis was laughing about it, while his heart yearned (for the child). And he returned; altogether returned.

Then the child grew; it became like that which it had (formerly) been. Then the Mantis came; while he came to look; and be in this manner walking came. While he came walking and looking, he espied the child, as the child was sitting in the sun. Then the child heard him, as be came rustling (along); the child sprang up, the child entered the water. And he looking stood, he went back. he went; he went to make for the child a front kaross (or apron), that and a | | *koroko.*¹ He put the things aside; then he put the front kaross (into a bag), that and the ||*koroko*; he in this manner went; he in this manner came he approached gently. And, as he approached gently, he espied the child lying in the sun, as the child lay yonder, in the sun, opposite the water. Therefore, he gently came up to the child. And the child heard him, as his father gently came. And the Mantis, when the child intended to get up, the Mantis sprang forward, he caught hold of the child. And he anointed the child with his scent; he anointed the child; be said: "Why art thou afraid of me? I am thy father; I who am the Mantis, I am here; thou art my son, thou art !gaunu-tsaxau; I am the Mantis, whose son thou art; the father is myself." And the child sat down, on account of it; and he took out the front kaross, he took out the ||*koroko*. He put the front kaross on to the child; he put the ||*koroko* on to the child; he put the front kaross on to the child. Then he took the child with him; they, in this manner, returning went; they returning arrived at home.

Then the young Ichneumon exclaimed: "What person can it be who comes with the Mantis?" And |*kuammang-a* replied: "Hast thou not just(?) heard that grandfather said he had gone to the baboons, while they were playing at ball there with the child's eye? while grandfather must have been playing before us; his son comes yonder with him! "And they returned, reaching the house. Then the young Ichneumon spoke; he said: "Why did my grandfather, the Mantis, first say that the

1. Another article for the child to wear.

baboons were those who killed the child, while the child is here Then the Mantis said: Hast thou not seen (that) he is not strong? while he feels that I came to put his eye into the water; while I wished that I might see whether the thing would not accomplish itself for me; therefore, I came to put his eye into the water. He came out of the water; therefore, thou seest (that) he is not strong. Therefore, I wished that I might wait, taking care of him; that I may see whether he will not become strong."

THE STORY OF THE LEOPARD TORTOISE.[1]

The people had gone hunting: she was ill; and she perceived a man [2] who came up to her hut; he had been hunting around.

She asked the man to rub her neck a little with fat for her; for, it ached. The man rubbed it with fat for her. And she altogether held the man firmly with it.[3] The man's hands altogether decayed away in it. [4]

Again, she espied another man, who came hunting. And she also spoke, she said.: "Rub me with fat a little."

And the man whose hands had decayed away in

1. *Testudo pardalis.*
2. The narrator explains that this misfortune happened to men of the Early Race.
3. By drawing in her neck.
4. The flesh decayed away and came off, as well as the skin and nails, leaving, the narrator says, merely the bones.

her neck, he was hiding his hands,[1] so that the other man should not perceive them, namely, that they had decayed away in it. And he said: "Yes; O my mate! rub our elder sister a little with fat; for, the moon has been cut,[2] while our elder sister lies ill. Thou shalt also rub our elder sister with fat." He was hiding his hands, so that the other one should not perceive them.

The Leopard Tortoise said Rubbing with fat, put (thy hands) into my neck. And he, rubbing with fat, put in his hands upon the Leopard Tortoise's neck; and the Leopard Tortoise drew in her head upon her neck; while his hands were altogether in her neck; and he dashed the Leopard Tortoise upon the ground, on account of it; while he desired, he thought, that he should, by dashing (it) upon the ground, break the Leopard Tortoise. And the Leopard Tortoise held him fast.

The other one had taken out his hands (from behind his back); and he exclaimed: "Feel (thou) that which I did also feel! "and he showed the other one his hands; and the other one's hands were altogether inside the Leopard Tortoise's neck. And he arose, he returned home. And the other one was dashing the Leopard Tortoise upon the ground; while he returning went; and he said that the other, one also felt what he had felt. A pleasant thing

1. He sat, putting his hands behind him, when the other man came, taking them out from the Leopard Tortise's neck.
2. The moon 'died', and another moon came, while she still lay ill, the narrator explains. "Whilst in the preceeding myths of the Mantis, the Moon, according to its origin, is only a piece of leather (a shoe of the Mantis),-in Bushman astrological mythology the Moon is looked upon as a man who incurrs the wrath of the Sun, and is consequently pierced by the knife (*i.e rays*) of the latter. This process is repeated until almost the whole of the Moon is cut away, and only one little piece left; which the Moon piteously implores the Sun to spare for his (the Moon's) children. (As mentioned above, the Moon is in Bushman mythology a male being.) From this little piece, the Moon gradually grows again until it becomes a full moon, when the Sun's stabbing and cutting processes recommence." ("A Brief Account of Bushman Folk-lore and other Texts." By W.H.I. Bleek, Ph.D. Cape Town, 1875. p. 9, §16.)

(it) was not, in which he had been! He yonder returning went; (he) arrived at home.

The people exclaimed: "Where hast thou been? And he, answering, said that the Leopard Tortoise had been the one in whose neck his hands had been; that was why he had not returned home, The people said: "Art thou a fool? Did not (thy) parents instruct thee? The Leopard Tortoise always seems as if she would die; while she is deceiving us."

II. SUN AND MOON.

THE CHILDREN ARE SENT TO THROW THE SLEEPING SUN INTO THE SKY.

The children were those who approached geutly to lift up the Sun-armpit, while the Sun-armpit lay sleeping.

The children felt that their mother was the one who spoke; therefore, the children went to the Sun; while the Sun shone, at the place where the Sun lay, sleeping lay.

Another old woman was the one who talked to the other about it; therefore, the other one spoke to the other one's children.[1] The other old woman said to the other, that, the other one's children should approach gently to lift up the Sun-armpit, that they should throw up the Sun-armpit, that the Bushman rice might become dry for them, that the Sun might make bright the whole place; while the Sun felt that the Sun went (along), it went over the whole sky, it made all places bright; therefore, it made all the ground bright; while it felt that the children were those who had coaxed (?) him; because an old woman was the one who spoke to the other about it, therefore, the other one said: "O children! ye must wait for the Sun, that the Sun may lie down to sleep, for, we are cold. Ye shall gently approach to lift

1. Another old woman was the one who said to the other, that the other should tell the other one's children; for, she (herself) had no young male children; for, the other was the one who had young male children who were clever, those who would understand nicely, when they went to that old man.

him up, while he lies asleep; ye shall take hold of him, all together, all together ye lift him up, that ye may throw him up into the sky."

They, in this manner, spoke; the old woman, in this manner, she spoke to the other; therefore, the other in this manner spoke to her, she also, in this manner, spoke to her children. The other said to her: "This (is the) story which I tell thee, ye must wait for the Sun."

The children came, the children went away; the old woman said: "Ye must go to sit down, when ye have looked at him, (to see) whether he lies looking; ye must go to sit down, while ye wait for him." Therefore, the children went to sit down, while the children waited for him; he lay down, he lifted up his elbow, his armpit shone upon the ground, as he lay. Therefore, the children threw him up into the sky,-while they felt that the old woman had spoken to them. The old woman said to the children: "O children going yonder! ye must speak to him, when ye throw him-up." The old woman said to the children: "O children going yonder! ye must tell him, that, he must altogether become the Sun, that he may go forward, while he feels that he is altogether the Sun, which is hot; therefore, the Bushman rice becomes dry, while he is hot, passing along in the sky; he is hot, while he stands above in the sky."

The old woman was the one who told the children about it, while she felt that her head was white; the children were listening to her, they were listening to their mamma, their mothex; their mother told them about it, that which the old woman in this manner said. Therefore, they thought in this manner. Therefore, they went to sit down. An older child spoke to another, therefore, they went to sit down, while they waited for him (the Sun), they went to sit down.

They arose, going on, they stealthily approached him, they stood still, they looked at him, they went forward; they stealthily reached him, they took hold of him) they all took hold of him together, lifted him up, they raised him, while he felt hot. Then, they threw him up, while he felt hot; they spoke to him while he felt hot: "O Sun! thou must altogether stand fast, thou must go along, thou must stand fast) while thou art hot."

The old woman said (that) they seemed to have thrown him up, he seemed to be standing fast above. They thus spoke, they in this manner spoke. Her (apparently the mother's) husband said: "The Suns' armpit is standing fast above yonder, he whom the children have thrown up; he lay, he intended to sleep; therefore, the children have thrown him up."

The children returned. Then, the children came (and) said: "(Our) companion who is here, he took hold of him, I also was taking hold of him; my younger brother was taking hold of him, my other younger brother was also taking bold of him; (our) companion who is here, his other younger brother was also taking hold of him. I said: 'Ye must grasp him firmly.' I, in this manner, spoke; I said: 'Throw ye him up!' Then, the children threw him up. I said to the children: 'Grasp ye the old man firmly!' I said to the children: 'Throw ye up the old man!' Then, the children threw up the old man; that old man, the Sun; while they felt that the old woman was the one who spoke."

An older child spoke, while he felt that he was a youth; the other also was a youth, they were young men (?), they went to throw up the Sun-armpit. They came to speak, the youth spoke, the youth talked to his grandmother: "O my grandmother! we threw him up, we told him, that, he should altogether become the Sun, which is hot; for, we are cold. We said: 'O my grandfather, Sun-armpit! Remain (at that) place; become thou the Sun which is hot; that the Bushman rice may dry for us; that thou mayst make the whole earth light; that the whole earth may become warm in the summer; that thou mayst altogether make heat. Therefore, thou must altogether shine, taking away the darkness; thou must come, the darkness go away.'"

The Sun comes, the darkness goes away, the Sun comes, the Sun sets, the darkness comes, the moon comes at night. The day breaks, the Sun comes out, the darkness goes away, the Sun comes. The moon comes out, the moon brightens the darkness, the darkness departs; the moon comes out, the moon shines, taking away the darkness; it goes along, it has made bright the darkness, it sets. The Sun comes out, the Sun follows (drives away?) the darkness, the Sun takes away the moon, the moon stands, the Sun pierces it, with the Sun's knife, as it stands; therefore, it decays away on account of it. Therefore, it says: "O Sun! leave for the children the backbone!" Therefore, the Sun leaves the backbone for the children; the Sun does so. Therefore, the Sun says that the Sun will leave the backbone for the children, while the Sun assents to him; the Sun leaves the backbone for the children; therefore, the moon painfully goes away, he painfully returns home, while he painfully goes along; therefore, the Sun desists, while he feels that the Sun has left for the children the backbone, while the Sun assents to him; therefore, the Sun leaves the backbone; while the Sun feels that the Sun assents to him; therefore, the Sun desists on account of it; he (the moon) painfully goes away, he painfully returns home; he again, he goes to become another moon, which is whole; he again, be lives; he again, be lives, while he feels that he had seemed to die. Therefore, he becomes a new moon; while he feels that he has again put on a stomach; he becomes large; while he feels that he is a moon which is whole; therefore, he is large; he comes, while he is alive. He goes along at night, he feels that he is the moon which goes by night, while he feels that he is a shoe[1]; therefore, he walks in the night.

The Sun is here, all the earth is bright; the Sun is here, the people walk while the place is light, the earth is light; the people perceive the bushes, they see the other people; they see the meat, which they are eating; they also see the springbok, they also head the springbok, in summer; they also head the ostrich, while they feel that the Sun shines; they also head the ostrich in summer; they are shooting the springbok in summer, while they feel that the Sun shines, they see the springbok; they also steal up to the gemsbok; they also steal up to the kudu, while they feel that the whole place is bright; they also visit each other, while they feel that the Sun shines, the earth also is bright, the Sun shines upon the path. They also travel in summer; they

1. The Mantis formerly, when inconvenienced by darkness, took off one of his shoes and threw it into the sky, ordering it to become the Moon.

are shooting in summer; they hunt in summer; they espy the springbok in summer; they go round to head the springbok; they lie down; they feel that they lie in a little house of bushes; they scratch up the earth in the little house of bushes, they lie down, while the springbok come.

FURTHER REMARKS.

The second version of the preceeding myth, which is unfortunately too long to be conveniently included in the present volume, contains a few interesting notes, furnished by the narrator,

||*kabbo* ("Dream"), which are given below. ||*kabbo* further explained that the Sun was a man; but, *not* one of the early race of people who preceded the Flat Bushmen in their country. He only gave forth brightness for a space around his own dwelling. Before the children threw him up, he had not been in the sky, but, had lived at his own house, on earth. As his shining had been confined to a certain space at, and round his own dwelling, the rest of the country seemed as if the sky were very cloudy; as it looks now, when the Sun is behind thick clouds. The sky was black (dark?). Thee shining came from one of the Sun's armpits, as he lay with one arm lifted up. When he put down his arm, darkness fell everywhere; when he lifted it up again, it was as if day came. In the day, the Sun's light used to be white; but, at night, it was red, like a fire. When the Sun was thrown up into the sky it became round, and never was a man afterwards.

TRANSLATION OF NOTES.

The First Bushmen[1] were those who first inhabited the earth. Therefore, their children were those who worked with the Sun. Therefore, the people who [later] inhabited their country, are those who say that the children worked, making the Sun to ascend, while they felt that their mothers had agreed together that they should throw up, for them, the Sun; that the Sun might warm the earth for them; that they-might feel the Sun's warmth, that they might be able to sit in the Sun.

1. The men of the early race.

When the first Bushmen had passed away, the Flat Bushmen inhabited their ground. Therefore, the Flat Bushmen taught their children about the stories of the First Bushmen.

The Sun had been a man, he talked; they all talked, also the other one, the Moon. Therefore, they used to live upon the earth; while they felt that they spoke. They do not talk, now that they live in the sky.

THE ORIGIN OF DEATH; PRECEDED BY A PRAYER ADDRESSED TO THE YOUNG MOON.

We, when the Moon has newly returned alive, when another person has shown us the Moon, we look towards the place at which the other has shown us the Moon, and, when we look thither, we perceive the Moon, and when we perceive it, we shut our eyes with our hands, we exclaim: "*!kabbi-a* yonder! Take my face yonder! Thou shalt give me thy face yonder! Thou shalt take my face yonder! That which does not feel pleasant. Thou shalt give me thy face,—(with) which thou, when thou hast died, thou dost again, living return, when we did not perceive thee, thou dost again lying down come,—that I may also resemble thee. For, the joy yonder, thou dost always possess it yonder, that is, that thou art wont again to return alive, when we did not perceive thee; while the hare told thee about it, that thou shouldst do thus. Thou didst formerly say, that we should also again return alive, when we died."

The hare was the one who thus did. He spoke, he said, that he would not be silent, for, his mother would not again living return; for his mother was altogether dead. Therefore, he would cry greatly for his mother.

The Moon replying, said to the hare about it that the hare should leave off crying; for, his mother was not altogether dead. For, his mother meant that she would again living return. The hare replying, said that he was not willing to be silent; for, he know that his mother would not again return alive. For, she was altogether dead.

And the Moon became angry about it, that the hare[1] spoke thus, while he did not assent to him (the Moon). And he hit with his fist, cleaving the hare's mouth; and while he hit the hare's mouth with his fist, he exclaimed: "This person, his mouth which is here, his mouth shall altogether be like this, even-when he is a hare;[2] he shall always bear a scar on his mouth; he shall spring away, he shall do-doubling (?) come back. The dogs shall chase him; they shall, when they have caught him, they shall grasping tear him to pieces,[3] he shall altogether die.

"And they who are men, they shall altogether dying go away, when they die.[4] For, he was not

1. It was a young male hare, the narrator explained.
2. The hare had also been a person; but, the Moon cursed him, ordering that he should altogether become a hare.
3. Or, bite, tearing him to pieces.
4. The people shall, when they die, they shall altogether dying go away; while they do not again living return. For the hare was the one who thus spoke; he said that his mother would not again living return.

willing to agree with me, when I told him about it, that he should not cry for his mother; for, his mother would again live; he said to me, that, his mother would not again living return. Therefore, he shall altogether become a hare. And the people, they shall altogether die. For, he was the one who said that his mother would not again living return. I said to him about it, that they (the people) should also be like me; that which I do; that I, when I am dead, I again living return. He contradicted me, when I had told him about it."

Therefore, our mothers said to me, that the hare was formerly a man; when he had acted in this manner, then it was that the Moon cursed him, that he should altogether become a hare. Our mothers told me, that, the hare has human flesh at his ||*katten-ttu*[1]; therefore, we, when we have killed a hare, when we intend to eat the hare, we take out the "biltong flesh"[2] yonder, which is human flesh, we leave it; while we feel that he who is the hare, his flesh it is not. For, flesh (belonging to) the time when he formerly was a man, it is.

Therefore, our mothers were not willing for us to eat that small piece of meat; while they felt that it is this piece of meat with which the hare was formerly a man. Our mothers said to us about it, did we not feel that our stomachs were uneasy if we

1. The meaning of ||*katten-ttu* is not yet clear; and the endeavors to obtain a hare, that it might be exactly ascertained from the Bushmen which piece of meat was meant,

were unsuccesful. The *ttu* at the end of the word shows that some sort of hollow of the human body is indicated.

Since these sheets have gone to press, Dr. J.N.W. Loubser, to whom I had applied for information regarding this particular piece of meat, was so good as to send me the following lines, accompanied by a diagram, which unfortunately it was already too late for me to include in the illustrations for this volume:—

"As regards the 'biltong flesh', I have often watched my mother cutting biltong, and know that each leg of beef contains really only one real biltong, *i.e.* the piece of flesh need not be cut into the usual oblong shape, bat has this *a priori*. In other words, it is a muscle of this form. From my anatomical knowledge I can only find it to correspond to the *musculus bicelis femoris* of the man. It will therefore be a muscle sitting rather high up the thigh (B of Figure)."

2. The narrator explained |*kuuii* to be "biltong flesh "(i.e., lean meat that can be cut into strips and sun-dried, making "biltong").

ate that little piece of meat, while we felt that it was human flesh; it is not hare's flesh; for, flesh which is still in the hare it is; while it feels that the hare was formerly a man. Therefore, it is still in the hare; while the hare's doings are those on account of which the Moon cursed us; that we should altogether die. For, we should, when we died, we should have again living returned; the hare was the one who did not assent to the Moon, when the Moon was willing to talk to him about it; he contradicted the Moon.

Therefore, the Moon spoke, he said: "Ye who are people, ye shall, when ye die, altogether dying vanish away. For, I said, that, ye should, when ye died, ye should again arise, ye should not altogether die. For, I, when I am dead, I again living return. I had intended, that, ye who are men, ye should also resemble me (and) do the things that I do; that I do not altogether dying go away. Ye, who are men, are those who did this deed; therefore, I had thought that I (would) give you joy. The hare, when I intended to tell him about it,—while I felt that I knew that the hare's mother had not really died, for, she slept,—the hare was the one who said to me, that his mother did not sleep; for, his mother had altogether died. These were the things that I became angry about; while I had thought that the hare would say: 'Yes; my mother is asleep.'"

For, on account of these things, he (the Moon) became angry with the hare; that the hare should have spoken in this manner, while the hare did not say: "Yes, my mother lies sleeping; she will presently arise." If the hare had assented to the Moon, then, we who are people, we should have resembled the Moon; for, the Moon had formerly said, that we should not altogether die. The hare's doings were those on account of which the Moon cursed us, and we die altogether; on account of the story which the hare was the one who told him. That story is the one on account of which we altogether die (and) go away; on account of the hare's doings; when he was the one who did not assent to the Moon; when the Moon intended to tell him about it; he contradicted the Moon, when the Moon intended to tell him about it.

The Moon spoke, saying that he (the hare) should lie upon a bare place; vermin should be those who were biting him, at the place where he was lying; he should not inhabit the bushes; for, he should lie upon a bare place; while he did not lie under a tree. He should be lying upon a bare place. Therefore, the hare is used, when he springs up, he goes along shaking his head; while he shakes out, making to fall the vermin from his head, in which the vermin had been hanging; while he feels that the vermin hung abundantly in his head. Therefore, he shakes his head, so that the other vermin may fall out for him.

(This, among the different versions of the Moon and Hare story called "The Origin of Death", has been selected on account of the prayer to the young Moon with which it begins.)

THE MOON IS NOT TO BE LOOKED AT WHEN GAME HAS BEEN SHOT.

We may not look at the Moon, when we have shot game; for, we look, lowering our head, while we do not look up, towards the sky; while we are afraid of the Moon's shining. It is that which we fear. For, our mothers used to tell us about it, that the Moon is not a good person, if we look at him.

For, if we look at him, when we have shot game, the beasts of prey will eat the game, when the game lies dying, if we look at the Moon. When the game does not die, the Moon's water is that which causes the game to live. For, our mothers used to tell us about it, that, the Moon's water yonder, (that) we see, which is on a bush, it resembles liquid honey. It is that which falls upon the game; the game arises, when it has fallen upon the game. It makes cool the poison with which we shot the game; and the game arises, it goes on, while it does not show signs of poison[1]; even if it had appeared as if it would die. The Moon's water is that which cures it. And it lives, on account of it.

Therefore, our mothers did not wish us to be looking about, we should not look at the things which are in the sky; while our mothers used to tell us about it, that the Moon, if we had looked at him, the game which we had shot, would also go along like the Moon, Our mothers said to us about it, did we

1. Literally, "make," or "become poison."

not see the Moon's manner of going? he was not in the habit of going to a place near at hand, for, the day was used to break, while he was still going along. The game would also do the same, if we had looked at the Moon. The day would break, while the game was still going along; while it resembled the Moon, at which we had looked. Therefore, we feared to look at the Moon; while we felt that our mothers used to tell us about it, that the game would desire to take us away to a place where no water was. We could (?) go to die of thirst, while it, leading us astray, took us away to a place where no water was.

THE GIRL OF THE EARLY RACE, WHO MADE STARS.[1]

My mother was the one who told me that the girl arose; she put her hands into the wood ashes; she threw up the wood ashes into the sky. She said to the wood ashes: "The wood ashes which are here, they must altogether become the Milky Way. They must white lie along in the sky, that the stars may stand outside of the Milky Way, while the Milky Way is the Milky Way, while it used to be wood ashes." They (the ashes) altogether become the Milky Way. The Milky Way must go round with the stars; while the Milky Way feels that, the Milky Way lies going round; while the stars sail along; therefore, the Milky Way, lying, goes along with the stars. The Milky Way, when the Milky Way stands upon the earth, the Milky Way turns across in front, while the Milky Way means to wait(?), While the Milky Way feels that the Stars are turning back; while the Stars feel that the Sun is the one who has turned back; he is upon his path; the Stars turn back; while they go to fetch the daybreak; that they may lie nicely, while the Milky Way lies nicely. The Stars shall also stand nicely around.

1. This girl is said to have been one of the people of the early race (*!Xwe- | na-ssho-!ke*) and the 'first' girl; and to have acted ill. She was finally shot by her husband. These *!Xwe- | na-ssho-!ke* are said to have been stupid, and not to have understood things well.

They shall sail along upon their footprints, which they, always sailing along, are following. While they feel that, they are the Stars which descend.

The Milky Way lying comes to its place, to which the girl threw up the wood ashes, that it may descend nicely; it had lying gone along, while it felt that it lay upon the sky. It had lying gone round, while it felt that the Stars also turned round. They turning round passed over the sky. The sky lies (still); the Stars are those which go along; while they feel that they sail. They had been setting; they had, again, been coming out; they had, sailing along, been following their footprints. They become white, when the Sun comes out. The Sun sets, they stand around above; while they feel that they did turning follow the Sun.

The darkness comes out; they (the Stars) wax red, while they had at first been white. They feel that they stand brightly around; that they may sail along; while they feel that it is night. Then, the people go by night; while they feel that the ground is made light. While they feel that the Stars shine a little. Darkness is upon the ground. The Milky Way gently glows; while it feels that it is wood ashes. Therefore, it gently glows. While it feels that the girl was the one who said that the Milky Way should give a little light for the people, that they might return home by night, in the middle of the night. For, the earth would not have been a little light, had not the Milky Way been there. It and the Stars.

The girl thought that she would throw up (into the air) roots of the *!huing*, in order that the *!huing* roots should become Stars; therefore, the Stars are red; while they feel that (they) are *!huing* roots.[1]

She first gently threw up wood ashes into the sky, that she might presently throw up *!huing* roots; while she felt that she was angry with her mother, because her mother had not given her many *!huing* roots, that she might eat abundantly; for, she was in the hut. She did not herself go out to seek food; that she might get(?) *!huing* for herself; that she might be bringing it (home) for herself; that she might eat; for, she was hungry; while she lay ill in the hut. Her mothers were those who went out. They were those who sought for food. They were 'bringing home *!huing*, that they might eat. She lay in her little hut, which her mother had made for her. Her stick stood there; because she did not yet dig out food. And, she was still in the hut. Her mother was the one who was bringing her food. That she might be eating, lying in the little hut; while her mother thought that she (the girl) did not eat the young men's game (ie. game killed by them). For, she ate the game of her father, who was an old man. While she thought that the hands of the young men would become cool. Then, the arrow would become cool. The arrow head which is at the top, it would be cold; while the arrow head felt that the bow was cold; while the bow felt that his

1. She threw up a scented root (eaten by some Bushmen) called !huing, which became stars; the red (or old) !huing making red stars, the white or young !huing making white stars. This root is, ||kabbo says, eaten by baboons and also by the porcupine.
   The same girl also made locusts, by throwing up into the sky the peel of the !kuissi [an edible root] which she was eating.
2. ||kabbo here explained that, when a girl has 'grown', she is put into a tiny hut, made by her mother, with a very small arpeture for the door; which her mother closes upon her. When she goes out, she looks upon the ground; and when she returns to the hut, she sits and looks down. She does not go far, or walk about at this time. When presently she becomes a, 'big girl', she is allowed to look about, and to look afar again; being, on the first occasion, allowed to look afar over her mother's hand. She leaves the small hut, when allowed to look about and around again; and she then walks about like the other women. During the time she is in retreat, she must not look at the springbok, lest they should become wild.

(the young man's) hands were cold. While the girl thought of her saliva, which, eating, she had put into the springbok meat; this saliva would go into the bow, the inside of the bow would become cool; she, in this manner, thought. Therefore, she feared the young men's game. Her father was the one from whom she alone ate (game). While she felt that she had worked (*i.e.* treated) her father's hands: she had worked, taking away her saliva (from them).

THE GREAT STAR, !GAUNU, WHICH, SINGING, NAMED THE STARS.

!gaunu,[1] he was formerly a great Star; therefore, his name is *!gaunu*, while he feels that he was the one who formerly spoke (lit. "called") the Stars' names; while he feels that he is a great one. Therefore, be called the Stars' names. Therefore, the Stars possess their names; while they feel that *!gaunu* was the one who called their names. He formerly sang, while he uttered the Stars' names. He said "||*Xwahai*"[2] to (some) Stars which are very small; they are those of which be made ||*Xwhai*; their small, fine ones are those which are ||*Xwhai*.

1. My (paternal) grandfather, |*Xugen-ddi*, was the one who told me star's stories."
2. The stars ||*Xwahai* |*aiti* and ||*Xwhai-@pua* were identified as "Altair" or "Alpha Aquilae", and "Gamma Aquilae", respectively, by the late Mr. George Maclear and Mr. Finlay of the Royal Observatory, on October 10, 1873, at Mowbray. ||*Xwhai gwai* was behind a tree and too low to be distinguished.

Therefore, the porcupine, when these Stars have, sitting, turned back, he will not remain on the hunting ground; for, be knows that it is dawn, when ||*Xwhai* has, lying, turned back. He returns home; for, he is used to look at these Stars; they are those which he watches; while he feels that he knows that the dawn's Stars they are.

WHAT THE STARS SAY, AND A PRAYER TO A STAR.

They (the Bushmen) wish, that they may also perceive things.[1] Therefore, they say that the Star shall take their heart, with which they do not a little hunger; the Star shall give them the Star's heart, the Star's heart,-with which the Star sits in plenty. For the Star is not small; the Star seems as if it had food. Therefore, they say, that the Star shall give them of the Star's heart, that they may not hunger.

The Stars are wont to call, "*Tsau! Tsau!*" therefore the Bushmen are wont to say, that the Stars curse for them the springboks' eyes; the Stars say, "*Tsau!*" they say, "*Tsau! Tsau!*" I am one who was listening to them. I questioned my grandfather (*Tsatsi*), what things it could be that spoke thus. My grandfather said to me that the Stars were those who spoke thus. The Stars were those who said, *Tsau!* while they cursed for the people

1. i.e. things which their dogs may kill.

the springboks' eyes. Therefore, when I grew up, I was listening to them. The Stars said, "*Tsau! Tsau!*" Summer is (the time) when they sound.

Because I used to sleep with my grandfather, I was the one who sat with my grandfather, when he sat in the coolness outside. Therefore) I questioned him, about the things which spoke thus. He said, the Stars were those who spoke thus; they cursed for the people the springboks' eyes.[1]

My grandfather used to speak to Canopus, when Canopus had newly come out; he said: "Thou shalt give me thy heart, with which thou dost sit in plenty, thou shalt take my heart,-my heart,-with which I am desperately hungry. That I might also be full, like thee. For, I hunger. For, thou seemest to be satisfied (with food);

hence thou art not small. For, I am hungry. Thou shalt give me thy stomach, with which thou art satisfied. Thou shalt take my stomach, that thou mayst also hunger. Give thou me also thy arm, thou shalt take my arm, with which I do not kill. For, I miss my aim. Thou shalt give me thy arm. For, my arm which is here, I miss my aim with it." He desired that the arrow might hit the springbok for him; hence, he wished the Star to give him the Star's arm, while the Star took his arm, with which he missed his aim.

He shut his mouth, he moved away, he sat down; while he felt that he wished to sit and sharpen an arrow.

1. I think that it was all the springbok.

!KO-G!NUING-TARA, WIFE OF THE DAWN'S-HEART STAR, JUPITER.

They sought for *!haken*,[1] they were digging out *!haken*. They went about, sifting *!haken*, while they were digging out *!haken*. And, when the larvæ of the, *!haken* were intending to go in (to the earth which was underneath the little hillock), they collected together, they sifted the larvæ of the *!haken* on the hunting ground.

And the hyena[2] took the blackened perspiration of her armpits, she put it into the *!haken*. And they[3] gave to *!ko-g!nuing-tara* of the *!hagen*. And *!ko-g!nuing-tara* exclaimed, she said to her younger sister: "Thou shalt leave this *!haken* alone; I will be the one who eats it. For, thou art the one who shalt take care of the child.[4] For, this *!haken*, its smell is not nice."

Therefore, as *!ko-g!nuing-tara* sat, eating the *!haken*,

1. *!haken* resembles "rice "(i.e. "Bushman rice "); its larvæ are like (those of) "Bushman rice". *!haken* is a thing to eat; there is nothing as nice as it is, when it is fresh.
2. A female hyena.
3. The hyenas (it) was, with the jackals, the blue cranes (and) the black crows.
4. It was *!ko-g!nuing-tara*'s child. The Dawn's-Heart was the one who buried the child away from his wife, under the *!huing* (a plant with a handsome green top, and little bulbous roots at the end of fibres in the ground. The roots are eaten by the Bushmen raw, and also roasted and made into meal, which is said to be excellent, |*hang#kass'o* thinks that the flower is red; but has not seen the plant since he was a child).

the ornaments[1] (ie., earrings, bracelets, leglets, anklets) of themselves) came off.[2] The kaross (skin cloak) also unloosened (itself), the kaross also sat down. The skin petticoat also unloosened (itself), the skin petticoat sat down. The shoes ilso unloosened (themselves). Therefore, she sprang up,[3] she in this manner trotted away. Her younger sister, shrieking, followed her.[4] She went; she went into the reeds. She went to sit in the reeds.

Her younger sister exclaimed: "O *!ko-g!nuing-tara*! wilt thou not first allow the child to suck?" And she (the elder sister) said: "Thou shalt bring it, that it may suck; I would altogether talk to thee, while my thinking-strings still stand." Therefore, she spoke., she said to her younger sister: "Thou must be quickly bringing the child, while I am still conscious; and thou shalt bring the child tomorrow morning."

Her younger sister returned home, also the hyena, when the hyena bad put on the ornaments; they returned home, while the Dawn's-Heart and the rest[5] were (still) out hunting. The Dawn's-Heart returned home, as the child cried there, while his younger sister-in-law was the one who had the child.

He came, he exclaimed: "Why is it, that *!ko-g!nuing-tara* is not attending to the child, while the child cries there?" The hyena did not speak.

1. Bracelet, anklet, leglet.
2. (They) came off, they sat down upon the ground.
3. She felt that she became a beast of prey.
4. Because she wanted to run to catch hold of her elder sister.
5. I think that he was with other people. I think that they seem to have been the jackals' husbands, and the quaggas, and the wildebeests with the ostriches.

|*Xe-dde-Yoe*[1] was soothing the child. She waited; her elder sister's husband went to hunt; and she took the child upon her back. She went to her elder sister; she walked, arriving at the reeds. She exclaimed: "O *!ko-g!nuing-tara*! let the child suck." And her elder sister sprang out of the reeds; her elder sister, in this manner, came running; her elder sister caught hold of her, she turning (her body on one side) gave her) elder sister the child. She said: "I am here" And her elder sister allowed the child to suck. She said: "Thou must quickly bring the child (again), while I am still conscious; for, I feel as if my thinking-strings would fall down." And her younger sister took the child upon her back, she returned home; while her elder sister went into the reeds.

And, near sunset, she went to her elder sister; while she felt that her elder sister was the one who had thus spoken to her about it; her elder sister said: "Thou must quickly bring the child, for, I feel. as if I should forget you, while I feel that I do not know." And, her younger sister took the child near sunset, she went to her elder sister, she stood. She exclaimed: "O !ko-g!nuing-tara! let the child suck." Her elder sister sprang out of the reeds; she ran up to her younger sister. And she caught hold of her younger sister. Her younger sister said: "I am here! I am here!" She allowed the child to suck. She said: "Thou must quickly come (again); for, I feel as if I should forget you, (as if) I should not any longer think of you." Her

1. The name of the younger sister of !ko-g!nuing-tara was |Xe-dde-Yoe. She was a (one of the early race).

younger sister returned home, while she went into the reeds.

Her younger sister, on the morrow, she went to her elder sister; she walked, coming, coming, coming, coming, she stood. And she exclaimed: "O !ko-g!nuing-tara!" let the child suck." And her elder sister sprang out of the reeds, she ran up to her younger sister, she caught hold of her younger sister. Her younger sister, springing aside, gave her the child. Her younger sister said: "I am here!" Therefore, she (the elder sister) spoke, she said to her younger sister: "Thou must not continue to come to me; for, I do not any longer feel that I know." And her younger sister returned home.

And they went to make a !ku[1] there (at the house). They played. The men played with them, while the women were those who clapped their hands, while the men were those who nodded their heads, while the women were those who clapped their hands for them. Then, the Dawn's-Heart, nodding his head, went up to his younger sister-in-law, he laid his hand on his younger sister-in-law (on her shoulder). Then his younger sister-in-law swerved aside. She exclaimed: "Leave me alone! your wives, the old she-hyenas,[2] may clap their hands for you."

Then the Dawn's-Heart ran to the hyena; he took

1. This is a dance or game of the Bushmen, which |hang#kass'o has not himself seen, but has heard of from Tuani-ang and #kammi, two of Tsatsi's wives. They used to say that their fathers made a !ku (and) played. Their mothers were those who clapped their hands, clapped their hands for the men; the men nodded their heads.
2. She said !gwai |e-tara, a from anger; anger was that on account of which she said !gwai |e-tara.

aim (with his assegai),[1] he pierced the place where the hyena had been sitting,[2] while the hyena sprang out, she trod, burning herself in the fire, while she sprang away; while the ornaments remained at the place where she had been sitting, and where she had been wearing them. She sprang away, while they remained.

And the Dawn's-Heart scolded his younger sister-in-law, why was it that his younger sister-in-law had not quickly told him about it; she had concealed from him about the hyena; as if this was not why he had seen that the woman had been sitting with her back towards bim, she had not been sitting with her face towards him. She had been sitting with her back towards him; the (*i.e.* his) wife had been sitting with her face towards him. A different person, she must be the one who was here, she had sat with her back towards him.[3] And he said that his younger sister-in-law should quickly explain to him about the place where the (his) wife seemed to be. His younger sister-in-law said: "Thou shalt wait, that the place may become light[4]; for, thou dost seem to think that (thy) wife is still like that which she used to be. We will go to (thy) wife, when the sun has come out."

1. (He) brought himself to a stand (in order to take aim).
2. She sat in the house, being afraid. Therefore, she took off the bracelets from her wrists, while she desired that she might sit quietly; while she felt that she left the things. She suspected that the people were making a *!ku* (on her account), therefore she did not go to the *!ku*, while she felt that she had been wearing *!ko-g!nuing-tara* things.
3. Because he had married the hyena, because he thought that it was *!ko-g!nuing-tara*.
4. Because it was night.

Therefore, on the morrow, he said that his younger sister-in-law must quickly allow them to go. Then his younger sister-in-law said: "We ought to drive, taking goats, that we may take goats to (thy) wife." Therefore, they drove, taking goats. They drove along goats, drove along goats; they took the goats to the reeds. And they drove the goats to a stand.[1]

|*Xe-dde-Yoe*[1] directed her elder sister's husband, she said that her elder sister's husband should stand behind her back, the other people must stand behind her elder sister's husband's back, while she must be the one to stand beside the goats. Then she exclaimed: *!ko-g!nuing-tara*! let the child suck."

Then her elder sister sprang out of the reeds; she, in this manner, she running came. She, when she had run to her younger sister, she perceived the goats, she turned aside to the goats. She caught hold of a goat. The Dawn's-Heart caught hold of (his) wife, while the wife caught hold of the goat; while his younger sister-in-law, |*Xe-dde-Yoe*, also took hold of the wife. All the people altogether caught hold of her. Other people were catching hold of the goats; they cut the goats open, they took out the contents of the stomach, they anointed *!ko-g!nuing-tara* with the contents of the stomachs. They, taking hold, rubbed off the hair[3] (from her skin). Therefore, when she sat down, she said: "Ye must, pulling, leave the hair on the tips of my ears; for, in that

1. They left off (driving), in order that the goats might stand still.
2. |*Xe* is a young girl. What the whole of |*Xe-dde-Yoe*'s name means, the narrator does not know.
3. The hair, with which she had become a lynx.

manner I shall come to hear; for, I do not feel as if I should hear." Therefore, the man (her husband), pulling off, left the hair on the tips of her ears, that hair which is thus[2] on the tips of the ears, standing on the top of them.

Therefore, the Dawn's-Heart used, when he was returning home,[3] to put an arrow on the bow, he walked, sticking the end of his assegai into the ground, as he returning came. His eyes were large, as he came walking along; they resembled fires. The people were afraid of him as he came, on account of his eyes; while they felt that his eyes resembled fires, as he came walking along. The jackals were afraid of him, as he returning came.

In order to throw more light on that portion of the story of *!ko-gnuing-tara* which is contained in the version here given, the following extract is supplied from page 11 of Dr. Bleek's "Second Report concerning Bushman Researches", printed at Cape Town, in 1875:—

"The "Dawn's-Heart" (the star Jupiter) has a daughter, who is identified with some neighboring star preceding Jupiter (at the time when we asked, it was Regulus or *Alpha* Leonis). Her name is the "Dawn's-Heart-child," and her relation to her father is somewhat mysterious. He calls her "my heart," he swallows her, then walks alone as the only Dawn's-Heart Star, and, when she is grown up, he spits her out again. She then herself becomes another (female) Dawn's-Heart, and spits out another Dawn's-Heart-child, which follows the male and female Dawn's-Heart. The mother of the latter, the first-mentioned Dawn's-Heart's wife, was the Lynx, who was then a beautiful woman, with a younger sister who carried her digging-stick after her. The Dawn's-Heart hid his child under the leaves of an edible root (*!kuissi*), where he thought that his wife would come and find it. Other animals and birds arrived first, and each proposed herself to the Dawn's-Heart-child as its mother; but they

1. She said that she should not hear, if all the hair were off her ears. Therefore, her husband should leave the other hair on her ears.
2. Holding up two fingers.
3. He always (henceforth) did thus, because the hyenas had made his heart angry, they had poisoned (his) wife.

were mocked at by the child, until at last it recognized its own mother. Among the insulted animals were the Jackal and the Hyena, who, to revenge themselves, bewitched the mother (Lynx) with some poisoned "Bushman rice" (so-called "ants' eggs"), by which means she was transformed into a lioness. la the dark, the Hyena tried to take her (the Lynx's) place in the hut, on the return of the Dawn's-Heart; but the imposture was made known to him by his sister-in-law. The Dawn's-Heart tried to stab the Hyena with his assegai, but missed her. She fled, putting her foot into the fire, and burning it severely. The bewitched wife was enticed out of the reeds by her younger sister, and then caught by her brothers, who pulled off the lion skin, so that she became a fair woman again. But, in consequence of having been bewitched by "Bushman rice," she could no longer eat that, and was changed into a lynx who ate meat.-This myth, which contains many minor, and some beautiful incidents, is partly given in the form of a narrative, and partly in discourses addressed by the Dawn's-Heart to his daughter, as well as in speeches made by the Hyena and her parents, after her flight home."

IIIA. OTHER MYTHS.

THE SON OF THE WIND.

The (son of the) Wind was formerly still. And he rolled[1] (a ball) to !na-ka-ti. He exclaimed: "O !na-ka-ti! There it goes!" And !na-ka-ti exclaimed: "O comrade! There it goes!" because inq-ka-ti felt that he did not know his (the other one's) name. Therefore, !na-ka-ti said: "O comrade! There it goes! "He who was the wind, be was the one who said: "O !na-ka-ti! There it goes!

Therefore, !na-ka-ti went to question his mother about the other one's name. He exclaimed: "O our mother! Utter for me comrade who is yonder, his name; for, comrade utters my name; I do not utter comrade's name. I would also utter comrade's name, when I am rolling (the ball) to him. For, I do not utter comrade's name; I would also utter his name, when I roll (the ball) to him." Therefore,

---

1. Rolled (a ball of) ||*kuarri* to him. I think that it must have been ||*kuarri*; for, ||*kuarri* is that with which we are rolling (a ball): when we wish to aim, seeing ourselves, whether a man aims better than the other people. Therefore, we are rolling (a ball) with ||*kuarri*.

    ||*kuarri* is found in our country. They stand in numbers around. Therefore, the porcupine eats them. We do not eat them; for they are poison.

2. The name !na-ka-ti |hang#kass'o was unable to explain. He thinks that it must have been given by the parents, as !na-ka-ti was still a child. He further stated that the word !na is the name of an insect which resembles the locust. It is large, and also resembles the *Acridium ruficorne*. It is red. It affects the eyes of the Bushmen. Their eyes become closed and they writhe with pain on account of the burning caused by this insect.

---

his mother exclaimed: "I will not utter to thee comrade's name. For, thou shalt wait; that father may first shelter for us the hut;[1] that father may first strongly shelter the hut.[2] And then I will utter for thee comrade's name. And thou shalt, when I have uttered for thee comrade's name, thou must, when I am the one who has uttered for thee comrade's name, thou must, when I have uttered for thee comrade's name, thou must scamper away, thou must run home, that thou mayest come into the hut, whilst thou dost feel that the wind would blow thee away."

Therefore, the child went; they (the two children) went to roll (the ball) there. Therefore, he (*!na-ka-ti*) again, he went to his mother, he again, he went to question his mother about the other one's name.

And his mother exclaimed: "|*erriten-!kuang-!kuang*" it is; *!gau-!gaubu-ti* it is. He is |*erriten-!kunag-!kunag*, he is *!gau-!gaubu-ti*, he is |*erriten-!kuang-!kuang*."

Therefore, *!na-ka-ti* went on account of it. He went to roll (the ball) there, while he did not utter the other one's name, while he felt that his mother was the one who had thus spoken to him. She said: "Thou must not, at first, utter comrade's name. Thou must, at first, be silent, even if comrade be the one who is uttering thy name. Therefore, thou shalt, when thou hast uttered comrade's name, thou must run home, while thou dost feel that the wind would blow thee away."

Therefore, *!na-ka-ti* went on account of it; they went to roll (the ball) there, while the other was

1. They had a hut . . . the hut was small. They probably had a mat hut.
2. That is, make a strong screen of bushes for the mat hut.

the one who uttered his (*!na-ka-ti*'s) name. While he (*!na-ka-ti*) felt that he wished that his father should first finish making the shelter for the hut. And (when) he saw that his father sat down, then he would, afterwards, utter the Other one's name, when he beheld that his father had finished sheltering the hut.

Therefore, when he beheld that his father had finished sheltering the hut, then he exclaimed: "There it goes! O |*erriten-!kuang-!kuang*! There it goes *!gau-!gaubu-ti*! There it goes! And he scampered away, he ran home; while the other one began to lean over, and the other one fell down. He lay kicking violently upon the vlei.[1] Therefore, the people's huts vanished away, the wind blew, breaking their (sheltering) bushes, together with the huts, while the people could not see for the dust. Therefore, his (the wind's) mother came out of the hut [2] (ie. of the wind's hut); his mother came, grasping (him), to raise him up; his mother, grasping (him), set him on his feet. And he was unwilling, (and) wanted to lie still. His mother, taking hold (of him), set him on his feet. Therefore, the wind became still; while the wind had, at first, while he lay, caused the dust to rise.

Therefore, we who are Bushmen, we are wont to say: "The wind seems to be lying down, for, it does not gently blow (i.e. it blows strongly). For, when it stands (upright), then it is still, when it stands; for, it seems to be lying down, when it

1. A depression in the ground, sometimes dry, sometimes covered with coarse grass and rushes, and sometimes filled with water.
2. Her hut remained standing, while it felt that they themselves were wind.

does in this manner. its knee is that which makes a noise, when it lies down; for its knee does sound. I had wished that it might gently blow for us, that we might go out, that we might ascend the place yonder, that we might behold the river bed yonder standing behind (the hill). For, we have driven away the spriugbok from this place. Therefore, the springbok, have gone to yonder (dry) river bed standing behind (the hill). For, we have not a little shot the springbok at this place; for, we have shot, letting the sun set,[1] at the springbok at this place."

1. Literally, "having put in the sun."

THE WIND.

The Wind [1] (i.e. the Wind's son) was formerly a man. He became a bird.[2] And he was flying, while he no longer walked, as he used to do; for, he was flying, and he dwelt, in the mountain (that is, in a mountain hole). Therefore, he was flying. He was formerly a man. Therefore, he was formerly rolling (a ball); he was shooting; while he felt that he was a person. He became a bird; and he was flying, and he dwelt in a mountain's hole. And he was coming out of it, he flew about, and) he returned to it. And he came to sleep in it; and, he early awaking goes out of it;

1. The young wind blew, while, the young wind felt that its fathers seemed formerly to have blown; for, they were the wind. Therefore, they blew. For the people did not tell me about the wind's parents—, for, they merely talked to me about the young wind.
2. The Wind was formerly a person; he, became a bird. Therefore, he is tied up in stuff. His skin is that which we call stuff.

he flies away, again, he flies away. And he again returns, while he feels that he has sought food. And he eats, about, about, about, about, he again returns. And he, again, comes to sleep (in) it.

[That this curious belief, that the wind now wears the form of a bird, was even lately in active existence among the Bushmen, the following will suffice to show:—]

Smoke's Man[1] was the one who formerly spoke to me about the wind, when he was still living with his master, Jacob Kotzé.[2] He said that the place at which he had seen the wind was Haarfontein;[3] while its Bushman name is *#koaXa*; while its name (by) which the Europeans call it, is Haarfontein.

Smoke's Man espied the wind at Haarfontein's mountain. Therefore, he was throwing a stone at the wind, while he believed (it) to be a *!kuerre!kuerre* (a cerfain bird). And the wind burst on account of it. Therefore, the wind did not blow gently; the wind raised the dust, because he had thrown a stone at the wind, The wind raised the dust, while the wind flew away. The wind went into a mountain's hole, and the wind burst; the wind did not gently blow.

And he (Smoke's Man), being afraid, went home; he went to sit under the hut's bushes,[4] while he

1. ||goo-ka-!kui, or "Witbooi Tooren", was the son of ||khabo ("Oud Jantje Tooren") and his wife, !kuabba-ang ("Oude Lies"). |han#kass'o used to teach "Witbooi" how to hunt springbok; being already grown up when "Witbooi" was still a child.
2. Jacob Kotzé is a Bastaard. He used to live at "Hartus Kloof".
3. Haarfontein's mountains in which he saw the Wind.
4. i.e. the bushes broken off and used to make a shelter for the mat hut.

did not look to the sheep. The sheep[1] by themselves, the sheep returning came, while he sat under the (hut's) bushes; while he felt that he did not perceive the sheep on account of the dust. Therefore, he went to sit under the (hut's) bushes, while he desired that the dust should settle for him, he sat under the (hut's) bushes, sat close under the hut's sheltering bushes, while he felt that he sat warming himself; while he felt that the place was cold. Therefore, he sat under the (hut's) bushes, while he felt that he sat warming himself. And he afterwards arose, he drove bringing the sheep[2] to the kraal, while he felt that the sun had met. Therefore he again, he went to sit under the (hut's) bushes, while he wished that his mother should be the one to bring him food.[3] Therefore, he came to sit under the (hut's) bushes, when he had brought the sheep to the kraal. He went to sit under the hut's bushes, while his mother who worked there,[4] she would be the one to bring him food. Therefore, he sat under the (hut's) bushes, while he desired that he might lie down.

Therefore, his mother worked (and) worked,[5]

1. The "Africander" sheep (those with the thick tails) will (|hang#kass'o says) return home alone; while the "Va'rland" sheep do not return home alone, but remain where they were left.
!k'oa is the name for "Va'rland sheep, or "Moff".
!gei s the name for "Africander sheep, "Kaap Schaap."
3. The sheep stand upon a bare (unenclosed) place, the Bastaard's sheep. Therefore, the shepherd dwells (ie. has his hut) on this side of the sheep; the wagon stands on that (the opposite) side of the sheep, while the sheep stand between.
4. He was (at that time) a child.
5. Worked at the master's, the Bastaard's.

his mother brought him food. Therefore, he ate up this little food, he lay down; while he felt that the Bastaards are not accustomed to give food liberally. "Silla" was the one who gave food liberally, Jacob Kotzés wife, while she felt that she was a Bushman (woman); she speaks the Bushman (language). We used, being satisfied, to leave the food which she gave to us. I used to live with her (i.e. at her place). Silla (and) Jacob Kotzé, they are those with whom I used to live.

#KAGA'RA[1] AND !HAUNU, WHO FOUGHT EACH OTHER WITH LIGHTNING.

They formerly, *#kagara* formerly went to fetch his younger sister, he went to take her away; he went to take her away from *!haunu*[2]; and he took (her) back to her parents.

!haunu gave chase to his brother-in-law, he passed along behind the hill.

The clouds came, clouds which were unequalled in beauty (lit. "clouds which not beautiful like them"); they vanished away.

#kagara said:[3] "Thou must walk on." His younger sister walked, carrying (a heavy burden of)

1 A bird (it) is; a little bird (it) is; it resembles the *Lanius Collaris* (a Butcher-Bird).
2. A man (it) is; the Rain (it) is. I think that a Rain's Sorcerer (he) seems to have been. His name resembles (that of) the mucus which we are used to blow out of our nose, which is thick, that which the Bushmen call *!hau!haung*.
3. To his younger sister.

things, (her) husband's things. He (*#kagara*) said: "Thou must walk on; for, home is not near at hand."

!haunu passed along behind (the hill).

The clouds came, the clouds vanished away.

#kagara said: "Thou must walk on, for, thou art the one who dost see." And he, because the house became near) he exclaimed: "Walk on! Walk on! "He waited for his younger sister; his younger sister came up to his side. He exclaimed: "What things can these be, which thou dost heavily carry?"

Then *!haunu* sneezed, on account of it;[3] blood poured out of his nostrils; he stealthily lightened at his brother-in-law. His brother-in-law fended him quickly off,[4] his brother-in-law also stealthily lightened at him. lie quickly fended off his brother-in-law. His brother-in-law also lightened at him. He (*#kagara*) said: "Thou must come (and) walk close beside me; for, thou art the one who dost see that husband does not allow us time; for, he does not singly lighten."

They (‡*kagara* and !*haunu*) went along angry with

1. The things which the wife carried, they resembled water; they, in this manner, were pushing at her; while they felt that they were not hard, they did in this manner (i.e. swayed forward), behind her back.
2. !*haunu* was the one from whose nostrils blood came out, when he intended to sneeze. He sneezed on account of his things, to which ‡*kagara* did in this manner (i.e. felt at roughly).
3. In the word ||*khabbe(t)* the *t* is barely pronounced. The meaning of this word is explained by the narrator as follows: (He) fends off his brother-in-law (by motioning with his arm). Fending off (it) is, when other people are fighting their fellows with their fists. Fending off is that which they are wont to do, they wave off with the arm, while they fend off the other one's arm. He (‡*kagara*) fended off the other one's lightning.

each other. !*haunu* had intended that he should be the one lightening to ‡*kagara* to whisk away

‡*kagara*. ‡*kagara* was one who was strong (lit. "was not light", or "did not feel light"), he continued to fend off his younger sister's husband, !*haunu*. His younger sister's husband was also lightening at him; he was lightening at his brother-in-law. Then he stealthily lightened at his younger sister's husband with black lightning,[1] he, lightening, whisked him up (and carried him to a little distance).

His younger sister's husband, in this manner, lay dying; he, in this manner, he thundered,[2] while ‡*kagara* bound up his head[3] with the net, he, returning, arrived at home.

He went to lie down in the hut, while !*haunu* lay thundering;[4] he thundered there, while ‡*kagara* went to lie down, when he had rubbed them (i.e. himself and his younger sister) with buchu,[5] buchu, buchu, buchu, he lay down.

1. Black lightning is that which kills us, that which we do not perceive it come; it resembles a gun, we are merely startled by the clouds' thundering, while the other man lies, shrivelled up lies.
2. As he lay.
3. His head ached; his head was splitting (with pain).
4. To thunder is !*kuerriten*; but the narrator explained that !*ke!keya* here means 'to lie thundering'; and illustrated the expression by saying that "the Bushmen are wont to say that the springbok is one which goes to lie bleating; it is not willing to die quickly".

5. Buchu (in Webster's international Dictionary of 1902) is stated to be, "A South African shrub (*Barosma*)".

Note by the Narrator.

My grandmothers used to say: "#*kagara* and his companion are those who fight in the East, he and !*haunu*."

When the clouds were thick, and the clouds, when the clouds were thick, and the clouds were at this place, and the clouds resembled a mountain, then, the clouds were lightening, on account of it. And my grandmothers used to say: "It is #*kagara*, with !*haunu*."

IV. ANIMAL FABLES.

THE HYENA'S REVENGE.

First Version.

The Hyena was the one who weut to the Lion's house, then, he deceived the Lion; while he felt that the Lion had acted grudgingly towards him about the quagga's flesh; therefore, the Lion came to the Hyena's house, when the Hyena was boiling there in the Hyena's pot; the Hyena boiled ostrich flesh in it.

Therefore, the Hyena gave soup to the Lion therefore, the Lion took hold of the pot, while the pot was hot; the Hyena also grasped the pot with his, hands; the Hyena said: "O Lion! Allow me to pour soup into the inside of thy mouth." The Hyena poured soup into the Lion's niouth; then, he put the mouth of the pot over the Lion's head, while the pot was hot; the soup was burning the Lion's eyes; the soup also burned the inside of his mouth. Then, he swallowed hot soup with his throat, he swallowed, causing himself to die with hot soup he died, while his head was inside the pot.

The Hyena took up the Hyena's stick, the Hyena was beating him with the stick, while his head was inside the pot; the Hyena was beating him; the Hyena struck, cleaving the pot asunder; while the Hyena felt that the Hyena had deceived him therefore, he came to the Hyena.

The Hyena killed him, with hot soup; while he felt that the pot had stood upon the fire; he took the pot off from the fire, while he felt that he intended to burn the Lion to death, with the soup's heat; while he felt that the Lion had been niggardly towards him about the quagga's flesh; therefore, he deceived him with the ostrich flesh; while he felt that he intended to put the Lion's head into the pot;

therefore, he deceived him; while he felt that (he had married a female Hyena, he also is a male Hyena; therefore, be is a "Decayed Arm",[1] on account of it.

The Lion also marries a Lioness, as the Lion is a male Lion. The Hyena also marries a female Hyena, as the Hyena is a male Hyena. The leopard also marries a leopardess, as the leopard is a male leopard. The hunting leopard[2] marries a hunting leopardess, as the hunting leopard is a male hunting leoparcl.

1. This expression is used to denote a person who acts ungenerously regarding food.
2. *Felis jubata.*

THE HYENA'S REVENGE.

Second Version.

The Hyena was the one who went to the Lion's house, then, the Lion acted grudgingly towards the Hyena; then, the Hyena became angry about it, therefore, the Hyena deceived the Lion, that he should also come to his house. The Hyena said: "O Lion! Thou must also visit my house; while he felt that he deceived the Lion; therefore, the Lion visited his house on account of it; he went to deceive the Lion with soup.

The Hyena said: "I am accustomed to pour soup into this child's mouth, I also pour soup into this child's mouth, I also pour soup into the child's mouth; I also pour into my wife's mouth soup."

Therefore, he poured soup into the Lion's mouth, he put the Lion's head into the pot, while he felt that he altogether put the Lion's head into the pot, that he might altogether kill the Lion with the soup's heat; while he feels that he is a Hyena who deceives other people; he speaks; therefore, he talked to the Lion about it. The Lion also speaks; they talked to each other; therefore, the Lion assented, because he also is a foolish Lion, because he is a Lion who kills people; he also eats people. The Hyena also kills people, while the Hyena feels that he also eats people; therefore, the Hyena carried off the old woman[1] on account of it.

Therefore, the Hyena took up the stick, he struck the Lion down, while the Lion's head was inside the pot; he beat him with the stick, while he felt that the Lion died, when his head was inside the pot.

1. This is an allusion to a favourite Bushman story. Vide §80 of Dr. Bleek's "Brief Account of Bushman Folklore and other Texts", Cape Town, 1875.

THE LION JEALOUS OF THE VOICE OF THE OSTRICH.

"It is the Story of the Lions and the Ostrich."

And the Lions conspired[1] together that they might deceive the Ostrich; for, the women[2] were

1. The Lion was a man, the Ostrich was also a man, at the time when the Lion kicked the Ostrich's ||*hatten-ttu,* when they called (in) the #*gebbi-ggu.* Therefore, the nail of the Ostrich decayed, while it felt that he (the Ostrich) had kicked the Lion's |*una-ttu.* Therefore, it decayed. Therefore, the people, with regard to the scar yonder on the Ostrich's ||*hatten-ttu,* they say that it is (from) the Lion's nail.
2. The women of the Ostriches and of the Lions.

wont, with regard to the Ostrich, they only praised the Ostrich for calling finely; the women did not praise them. And they (the Lions), speaking, said: "In what manner shal I we deceive?" And another Lion answered, he said: "We must tell the women to make a (game of) #*gebbi-ggu,*[1] that we may see whether the women will again do as they are wont to do; when they only admire (?) the Ostrich; that we may really see whether it be true that the women admire (?) the Ostrich. We shall see what the Ostrich will do." And another Lion spoke, be said: "Why can it be that the Ostrich calls so well (lit. does not a little call sweetly)?" And the other Lion answered, he said: "The ostrich calls with his lungs; therefore, his throat sounds in this manner; his chest's front. Thou dost call with thy mouth; therefore, thou dost not call nicely."

The other Lion answered, he said: "Ye must make a (game of) #*gebbi-ggu,* that ye may kill the Ostrich, that ye may take out the Ostrich's lungs,

1. The |*goo* or #*gebbi-ggu* among the Grass Bushmen.

> They (the Grass Bushmen) call [like the male ostrich]; the women clap their hands for them; they (the men) call to the women. The women are those who dance; they (the men) call. And this woman goes out (from the dance), she stands [being weary], while two other persons (ie. two other women), they come forward in among the men, while the men call. They call more sweetly than anybody, for, their throats sound like real Ostriches; while the women are those who sing, while the men call.

that ye may eat them; and ye will call, sounding like the Ostrich, when ye have eaten the Ostrich's lungs."

And the Lions spoke, they said to the women: "Make a (game of) #*gebbi-ggu*" They would listen whether it were true that the Ostrich calls finely.

And the women made a (game of) #*gebbi-ggu* on account of it; and the Lion called. The Ostrich was still yonder at his house; the Lion called; the women did not applaud the Lion, because they felt that the Lion did not call well; for, they continued to look at the Lion; and the Ostrich came; and the Ostrich called, sounding afar. And the women exclaimed: "I do wish that the Lion called in this manner; for, he sounds as if he had put his tail into his mouth, while the Ostrich calls in a resounding manner."

And the Lion, answering, said: "Dost thou not see that the women act in this manner towards the Ostrich? and it is only the Ostrich whom they cherish, because he possesses this sweet call. The women cherish him only."

And the other Lion became angry on account of it; namely, that the Ostrich was the one whom the women cherished; and he seemed as if he were about to move away; and he scratched the Ostrich's ||*hatten-ttu*, scratched, tearing it. And he called out: "is it a thing which calls sweetly?" while he kicked the Ostrich's ||*hatten-ttu*. And the Ostrich also quickly (?) turned back. And the Ostrich also kicked, tearing his |*uan-ttu*; and the Ostrich, speaking, said: "This person, it is his |*uan-ttu*, he is wroth with me, because he is the one who is wont to hold his tail in his mouth

when he calls; this is why the women do not praise him; while the women feel that he does not call nicely for the women. This is why the women are not willing to make a #*gebbi-ggu* for him; the women feel that he does not call, sounding like me; in that case the women would have praised him."

Therefore, my grandfather spoke, he said to us[1] about it, that we should also do as the Lion formerly did to the Ostrich about it, when he had formerly killed the Ostrich; he ate the Ostrich's lungs, while he wished that he might call, sounding like the Ostrich. Therefore, he ate the lungs.

My grandfather also gave us the Ostrich's lungs to eat, that we might also resemble the Ostrich; and we spoke, we asked our grandfather, whether we should not baking cook the Ostrich's lungs; and our grandfather spoke, he said to us about it, that we should not cook the Ostrich's lungs; for, we in this manner eat the Ostrich's lungs, eat them raw. For, we should, if we were to eat the Ostrich's lungs when they were cooked, we should not call, sounding like the Ostrich, if we ate them when they were cooked. Our grandfather, speaking, told us about it, that, we should not chew the Ostrich's lungs, we should swallow them down, while they were whole. For, we should, if we had chewed the Ostrich's lungs, we should not call, sounding like the Ostrich, if we had chewed them.

And, our grandfather, speaking, said: "Ye must come and stand around, that I may be cutting off from the Ostrich's lungs, that I may be giving

1. We who were little boys," the narrator explains.

them to you, that ye may be swallowing them down." And we, answering, said: "O my grandfather! We do not wish to eat the Ostrich's lungs when they are raw. "And our grandfather answered, he said to us about it, that we also wished to resemble the Lion; he formerly became angry with the Ostrich, about the Ostrich's fine calling. We also should be wont if we heard that our companions called, sounding very sweetly, we should become angry with our companions, when we heard that they called, sounding very sweetly; we should fight with them, if we felt that the women did not applaud (?) us. Therefore, we become angry. We are fighting with them, because we are angry that the women do not applaud(?) us.

Translation of Notes.

The Lion was a man, the Ostrich was also a man, at that time when the Lion kicked the Ostrich's ||*hatten-ttu*; when they were calling the #*gebbi-ggu*. Therefore, the nail of the Ostrich decayed;

while it felt that he had kicked the Lion's |*uan-ttu*. Therefore, it decayed on account of it. Therefore, the people are used to say to the scar which is yonder upon the Ostrich's ||*hatten-ttu*, that it is the Lion's nail.

The time when the Lion had not killed the Ostrich, was the one at which they made the ǂ*gebbi-ggu*'s fight. He, afterwards, killed the Ostrich; and he ate the Ostrich; it was at a new time that he ate the Ostrich; and he made "a food's thing" of the Ostrich; therefore, the old people say, that, the Lion is a thing which is wont, when it has killed an Ostrich, it is not willing to go away in fear, leaving the Ostrich; for, it is wont, even if we are speaking very angrily to it, it is not willing to go away in fear, leaving the Ostrich. For, it would be very angry with us, if we even thought that we would drive it away.

THE RESURRECTION OF THE OSTRICH.

The Bushman kills an Ostrich at the Ostrich's eggs; he carries away the Ostrich to the house. And his wife takes off the Ostrich's short feathers which were inside the net, because they were bloody; she goes to place them (on the bushes). They eat the Ostrich meat.

A little whirlwind comes to them; it blows up the Ostrich feathers. A little Ostrich feather that has blood upon it, it blows up the little feather into the sky. The little feather falls down out of the sky, it having whirled round falls down, it goes into the water, it becomes wet in the water, it is conscious, it lies in the water, it becomes Ostrich flesh; it gets feathers, it puts on its Wings, it gets its legs, while it lies in the water. It walks out of the water, it basks in the sun upon the water's edge, because it is still a young Ostrich. Its feathers are young feathers (quills); because its feathers are little feathers. They are black; for a little male Ostrich it is. He dries (his feathers) lying upon the water's bank, that he may afterwards walk away, when his little feathers are dried, that he may walk unstiffening his legs. For he had been in the water; that he may walk strengthening his feet, for he thinks that his feet must be in (Ostrich's) veldschoens, because his feet become strong. While he walks strengthening his feet) he lies down, he hardens his breast, that his breastbone may become bone. He walks away, he eats young, bushes, because a young Ostrich he is. He swallows young plants which are small, because a little Ostrich he is. His little feather it was which became the Ostrich, it was that which the wind blew up, while the wind was a little whirlwind; he thinks of the place on which he has scratched; he lets himself grow, that he may first be grown, that he may afterwards, lying (by the way), go to his house's old place, where he did die lying there, that he may go to scratch in the old house,[1] while he goes to fetch his wives. He will add (to the two previous ones)

1. Making the new house on the old one.

another she Ostrich; because he did die, he will marry three Ostrich wives. Because his breastbone is bone, he roars, hardening his ribs, that his ribs may become bone. Then he scratches (out a house), for he does sleeping (by the way) arrive at the house's place; he roaring calls the Ostrich wives, that the Ostrich wives may come to him. Therefore he roaring calls, that he may perceive the she Ostriches come to him; and he meets them, that he may run round the females; for he had been dead; he dying left his wives. He will look at his wives' feathers, for his wives' feathers appear to be fine.

When he has strengthened his flesh, he feels heavy, as he comes, because his legs are big, his knees are large; he has grown great feathers, because the quills are those which are great feathers; these feathers become strong, they are old feathers. Therefore he roars strongly, for the ribs are big. And he is a grown up Ostrich; his wings' feathers are long. He thinks that he will scratch, that the females may lay eggs; for his claws are hard, they want to scratch for he brings the females to the house's place. The females stand eating. Therefore he goes back, he scratches, while the she Ostriches ea:t there. He first goes to scratch drying the house, because it is damp, that the iuside of the house may dry. The she Ostriches shall look at the house; one she Ostrich, she lies down to try the house, she tries whether the house seems to be nice; she first sleeps opposite the house, because the inside of the house is wet, as the rain has newly fallen. Thus they first lie opposite the house, they sleep opposite the house. She shall lie, making the ground inside the house soft; she first lies, making the ground inside the house soft, that the inside of the house may be dry, that another female may come and lay an egg in the inside of the house which is dry, for the earth of the house is wet. She first goes to lie opposite the house. One other female again comes, She comes to lay another new egg; she first comes to flap her wings in the house, for two small eggs stand (there); she again goes to sleep opposite the house. All the females are those who sleep at the house. He galloping in the dark drives the females to the house; he shall running take the females to the house; they

all walking arrive at the house. Another female, a different one, lays another egg; they again flapping their wings peck at it. He drives the females away; he lies inside the house. These females, following each other, reach him at the house; these females send him off, they all lay eggs. He goes, for he goes away to eat. Two wives lie in the house; another wife also goes with him, they go to eat together; they sleep. The two wives sleep in the house. They two (the male and female) return early, they shall early send off the two wives, who had lain in the house. The wife who had been with him, lays another egg; the wives go, all the wives, whilst he lies down, that he may sleep at the house. He will drive away the jackal, when he thinks that the jackal is coming to the eggs, the jackal will push the eggs. Therefore he takes care of the eggs, because his children they indeed are. Therefore, he also takes care of them, that he may drive away the jackal, that the jackal may not kill his children, that he may kick the jackal with his feet.

THE VULTURES, THEIR ELDER SISTER, AND HER HUSBAND.

The Vultures formerly made their elder sister of a person;[1] they lived with her.

They, when their elder sister's husband[2] brought (home) a springbok, they ate up the springbok. And their elder sister's husband cursed them, he scolded at them.

And their[3] elder sister took up the skin of the springbok, she singed it. Their elder sister boiled the skin of the springbok, their elder sister took it out (of the pot).

1. A woman was the one of whom they made their elder sister. The woman was a person of the early race.
2. man of the early race (he) was.
3. |han#kass'o explains the use of the singular form of the pronoun, here, in the following manner: "Their elder sister was one, they were many."

And they were taking hold[1] of the pieces of skin, they swallowed them down. Their elder sister's husband scolded them, because they again, they ate with their elder sister, of the springbok's skin, when they had just eaten the body of the springbok, they again, they ate with their elder sister of the springbok's skin.

And they were afraid of their elder sister's husband, they went away, they went in all directions, they, in this manner, sat down. And they looked at their elder sister's husband, they were looking furtively at their elder sister's husband.

Their elder sister's husband went hunting. He again, he went (and) killed a springbok; he brought the springbok home, slung upon his back.[3] They again, they came (and) ate up the springbok. Their elder sister's husband scolded them. And they moved away, they sat down. [4]

Their elder sister singed the springbok's skin she boiled the springbok's skin. Their elder sister was giving to them pieces of the skin, they were swallowing them down.

Therefore, on the morrow, their elder sister's husband said that his wife must go with him; she should altogether eat on the hunting ground; for, his younger sisters-in-law were in the habit of eating up the springbok. Therefore, the wife should go with him. Then, the wife went with him.

1. I think that it was (with) their hands, if they were not taking hold of things with their mouths; for, they flew.
2. Their elder sister was the one who had been giving to them of the springbok's skin.
3. Carried the springbok.
4. When the meat was finished; they had eaten up the meat.

Therefore, they,[1] when their elder sister had gone, they went out of the house,[2] they sat down opposite to the house,[3] and they conspired together about it. They said, this other one said: "Thou shalt ascend, and then thou must come to tell us what the place seems to be like." And another said: "Little sister[4] shall be the one to try; and then, she must tell us." And then, a Vulture who was a little Vulture girl, she arose, she ascended.

They said: "Allow us, that we may see what little sister will do." Then, she went, disappearing in the sky, they no longer perceived her.

They sat; they were awaiting the time at which their younger sister should descend. Then, their younger sister descended (lit. fell) from above out of the sky, she (came and) sat in the midst of them.

And they exclaimed Ah! What is the place like? "And their younger sister said: "Our mate[5] who is here shall ascend, that she may look. For, the place seems as if we should perceive a thing, when we are above there."

Then, her elder sister who was a grown up girl, she arose, she ascended, she went, disappearing in

1. The Vultures.
2. Their elder sister's house, in which they had been living with their elder sister.
3. They felt that they were people.
4. A little girl.
5. Her elder sister was the one of whom she spoke.

the sky. She descended from above, she sat in the midst of the other people. [1]

And the other people said: "What is the place like?" And she said: "There is nothing the matter with the place; for, the place is clear. The place is very beautiful; for, I do behold the whole place; the stems of the trees,[2] I do behold them; the place seems as if we should perceive a springbok, if a springbok were lying under a tree; for the place is very beautiful."

Then, they altogether arose, all of them, they ascended into the sky,[3] while they wished that their elder sister should eat; for, their elder sister's husband scolded them.

Therefore, they used, when they espied their elder sister's husband coming, they ate in great haste. They said: "Ye must eat! ye must eat! ye must eat in great haste! for, that accursed man who comes yonder, he could not endure us." And, they finished the springbok, they flew away, flew heavily away, they thus, they yonder alighted; while their elder sister's husband came to pick up the bones.

They, when they perceived a springbok, they descended, and their elder sister perceived them, their elder sister followed them up.[4] They ate, (they) ate, they were looking around; they said: "Ye must eat; ye should look around; ye shall leave some meat for (our) elder sister; ye shall

1. The Vultures.
2. Large trees.
3. While they felt that they altogether became Vultures.
4. Vultures are those which we follow up.

leave for (our) elder sister the undercut,[1] when ye see that (our) elder sister is the one who comes." And they perceived their older sister coming, they exclaimed: "Elder sister really seems to be coming yonder, ye must leave the meat which is in the springbok's skin."[2] And, they left (it).[3] And, when they beheld that their elder sister drew near to them, they went away, they went in all directions.

Their elder sister said: "Fie! how can ye act in this manner towards me? as if I had been the one who scolded you!"

And their elder sister came up to the springbok, she[3] took up the springbok, she returned home; while the Vultures went forward

(?), they went to fly about, while they sought for another springbok, which they intended again to eat.

1. It is meat; the |*kuaiten* is that which lies along the front of the upper part of the spine.
2. The word |*kuaiten*, translated here as "undercut "(in accordance with the description of its position), bears some resemblance to that given for "biltong flesh", in the Katkop dialect, by *Dia!kwnain*, which is |*kwaii*.
3. They ate the skin together (with the meat).
4. It is possible that the pronoun *hi* may have combined with the verb here.

DDI-XERRETEN, THE LIONESS, AND THE CHILDREN.

Ddi-Xerreten,[1] formerly, when the Lioness was at the water, dipping up,[2] (when) she had gone to dip[3]

1. Their elder sister, the Vultures' elder sister.
2. A man of the early race he was. His head was stone.
3. I think that she probably dipped up water with a gemsbok's stomach; for she killed gemsbok.

up water there, *Dai-Xerreten* felt that the Lioness was the one who had gathered together the people's children, because the Lioness felt that she was an invalid on account of (her) chest; therefore, she gathered together the people's children, that the children might live with her, that the children might work for her; for, she was an invalid, and she could not do hard work.

Therefore, *Dai-Xerreten* went to her house, when she was dipping up water. *Dai-Xerreten* went in her absence to the house, *Dai-Xerreten* went to the children, at the house. *Dai-Xerreten* went to the house reaching the children. *Dai-Xerreten* sat down. And *Dai-Xerreten* said: "O children sitting here! The fire of your people is that which is at the top of the ravine which comes down from the top (of the hill)." Therefore, two children arose, they went away to their own people.

Dai-Xerreten again said: "O children sitting here! The fire of your people is that which is below the top of the ravine which comes down on this side (of the hill)." And three children[1] thus went, while they went away to their own people.

And he again said: "O little child sitting here! Thy people's fire is that which is below the top of the ravine which comes down on this side (of the hill)." And the child arose, it thus went, while the child went away to its own people.

He again said: "O children sitting here! The fire of your people is that which is below[2] the top

1. Literally, "children which became three."
2. because the house is in the ravine (i.e., not where the water flows, but among the bushes).

of the ravine[1] which comes down on this side (of the hill)." And two children arose, they thus went away, while they went away to their own people.

And he again said: "O children sitting here! Your people's fire is that which is at the top. of the ravine which comes down from the top (of the hill)." And two children arose, they thus went away.

And he again said: "O children sitting here! The fire of your people is that which is at the top of the ravine which comes down from the top (of the hill)." And three children arose, they thus went away; while they went away to their own people.

And he again said: "O children sitting here![2] The fire of your people is that which is at the top of the ravine which comes down from the top (of the hill)." And two children arose, they thus went away; while they went away to their own people; while *Dai-Xerreten* sat waiting for the Lioness.

And the Lioness came from the water, she thus returning came. She came along looking (at the house); she did not perceive the children. And she exclaimed: "Why do the children (stammering with rage) children children children, the children not do so to me? and the children do not play here, as they are wont to do? It must be this man who sits at the house; his head resembles *Dai-Xerreten*."[3]

And she became angry about it, when she perceived

1. He speaks of another ravine.
2. Her children were not there; for the people's children were those whom she had.
3. She recognized him.

Dai-Xerreten.[1] She exclaimed: "*Dai-Xerreten* indeed (?) sits here!" She walked up to the house. She exclaimed: "Where are my children?"[2] And *Dai-Xerreten* said: Our children (they) are not." And the Lioness exclaimed: "Out on thee! leave off! thou must give me the children!" *Dai-Xerreten* said: "Our children (they) were not."

And the Lioness caught hold of his head. She exclaimed: "*Xabbabbu*"[3] (growling) to the other one's head. And she exclaimed: "Oh! Oh dear! Oh dear! Oh dear! Oh dear! my teeth! This must be why this cursed(?) man's big head came to sit in front of my house!" While *Dai-Xerreten* said: "I told thee that our children they were not." The Lioness exclaimed: "Destruction! Thou hast been the one whose big head came to sit (here)." Our children[4] (they) were not."

And he arose, he returned (home); while the Lioness sat in anger at her house; because he had come (and) taken away from her the children, who had been (living) peacefully with her; for she felt that she had done well towards the children; she did not a little love the children while she was doing so.

1. Because she did not perceive the children.
2. The narrator's translation of |*ne* |*auwaki !kauken* was "Where are my children?" but "Give me the children" or "Show me the children "may be verbally more accurate.
3. Growling put in the head.
4. *Dai-Xerreten* was the one who spoke thus.

THE MASON WASP[1] AND HIS WIFE.

The Mason Wasp[2] formerly did thus as he walked along, while (his) wife walked behind him, the wife said: "O my husband! Shoot for me that hare!" And the Mason Wasp laid down his quiver; the Mason Wasp said: "Where is the hare? And (his) wife said: The hare lies there."

And the Mason Wasp took out an arrow; the Mason Wasp in this manner went stooping along.[3] And the wife said: "Put down (thy) kaross! Why is it that thou art not willing to put down (thy) kaross? "Therefore, the Mason Wasp, walking along, unloosened the strings of the kaross; he put down the kaross. Therefore the wife said: "Canst thou be like this?[4] This must have been why thou wert not willing to lay down the kaross."

Therefore, the Mason Wasp walked, turning to one side; he aimed at (his) wife, he shot, hitting the (head of) the arrow on (his) wife's breast[5] (bone).

1. The Mason Wasp resembles the *Palpares* and *Libellula*. It has a small body. The Mason Wasp flies, and is to be seen in summer near water; |*hang#kass'o* has seen it in our garden at Mowbray. it is rather smaller than the *Palpares* and *Libellula*.
2. He was formerly a man; therefore, he had a bow; therefore, he shot his wife, when he had not shot the hare.
3. We are accustomed to go along stooping, when we wish that the hare may quietly lie hidden (knowing that people are at hand; lying still, thinking that it will be passed by).
4. She mocked at the man on account of the middle of the man's body, which was slender; hence she mocked at the man.
5. *i.e.* breaking her breastbone.

And (his) wife fell down dead on account of it. Then he exclaimed: "*Yi ii hihi*! O my wife *hi*! "(crying) as if he had not been the one to shoot (his) wife. He cried, that he should have done thus, have shot his wife; his wife died.

V. LEGENDS.

THE YOUNG MAN OF THE ANCIENT RACE, WHO WAS CARRIED OFF BY A LION; WHEN ASLEEP IN THE FIELD.

A young man[1] was the one who, formerly hunting, ascended a hill; he became sleepy; while he sat looking around (for game), he became sleepy. And he thought that he would first lie down; for he was not a little sleepy. For what could have happened to him today? because he had not previously felt like this.[2]

And he lay down on account of it; and he slept, while a lion came; it went to the water,[3] because the noonday (heat) had "killed" it; it was thirsty; and it espied the man lying asleep; and it took up the man.

And the man awoke startled; and he saw that it was a lion which had taken him up. And he thought that he would not stir; for the lion would biting kill him, if he stirred; he would first see what the lion intended to do; for the lion appeared to think that he was dead.

And the lion carried him to a zwart-storm tree[3]; and the lion laid him in. it.[4] And the lion

1. He was a young man of the early race.
2. It is evident, from another version of this legend, given by !kweiten ta | |ken (VI.-2, pp. 4014-4025), that the unusual sleepiness is supposed to be caused by the lion.
3. To a water pit.
4. This is described by the narrator as being a large tree, which has yellow flowers and no thorns.
5. The lion put the man half into the tree, at the bottom of it; his legs were not in it.

thought that it would (continue to) be thirsty if it ate the man; it would first go to the water, that it might go to drink; it would come afterwards to eat, when it had drunk; for, it would (continue to) be thirsty if it ate.

And it trod, (pressing) in the man's head between the stems of the zwart-storm tree; and it went back. And the man turned his head a little.[1] And the lion looked back on account of it; namely, why had the nian's head moved? when it had first thought that it had trodden, firmly fixing the man's head. And the lion thought that it did not seem to have laid the man nicely; for, the man fell over. And it again trod, pressing the man's head into the middle (of the stems) of the zwart-storm tree. And it licked the man's eyes' tears.[2] And the man wept; hence it licked the rnan's eyes. And the man felt that a stick[3] did not a little pierce the hollow at the back of his head; and the man turned his head a little, while he looked steadfastly[4] at the lion, he turned his head a little. And the lion looked (to see) why it was that the thing seemed as if the man had moved. And it licked the man's eyes' tears. And the lion thought it would tread, thoroughly pressing down the man's head, that it might really see whether it had been the one who had not laid the man

1. The tree hurt the back of the man's head; therefore he moved it a little.
2. The man cried quietly, because he saw himself in the lion's power, and in great danger.
3. Narrator explains that the stick was one of those pieces that had broken off, fallen down, and lodged in the bottom of the tree.
4. The man looked through almost closed eyes; but watched to see if the lion rcmarked that be moved his head.

down nicely. For, the thing seemed as if the man had stirred. And the man saw that the thing seemed as if the lion suspected that he was alive; and he did not stir, although the stick was piercing him. And the lion saw that the thing appeared as if it had laid the man down nicely; for the man did not stir; and it went a few steps away, and it looked towards the man, while the man drew up his eyes; he looked through his eyelashes; he saw what the lion was doing. And the lion went away, ascending the hill; and the lion descended (the hill on the other side), while the man gently turned his head because he wanted to see whether the lion had really gone away. And he saw that the lion appeared to have descended (the hill on the other side); and he perceived that the lion again (raising its head) stood peeping behind the top of the hill;[1] because the lion thought that the thing had seemed as if the man were alive; therefore, it first wanted again to look thoroughly. For, it seemed as if the man had intended to arise; for, it had thought that the man had been feigning death. And it saw that the man was still lying down; and it thought that it would quickly run to the water, that it might go to drink, that it might again quickly come out (from the water), that it might come to eat. For, it was hungry; it was one who was not a little thirsty; therefore, it first intended to go to drink, that it might come afterwards to eat, when it had drunk.

The man lay looking at it, at that which it did;

1. The lion came back a little way (after having gone out of sight) to look again.

and the man saw that its head's[1] turning away (and disappearing), with which it turned away (and disappeared), seemed as if it had altogether gone. And the man thought that he would first lie still, that he might see whether the lion would not again come peeping. For, it is a thing which is cunning; it would intend to deceive him, that the thing might seem (as if) it had really gone away; while it thought that he would arise; for, he had seemed as if he stirred. For, it did not know why the man had, when it thought that it had laid the man down nicely, the man had been falling over. Therefore, it thought that it would quickly run, that it might quickly come, that it might come to look whether the man still lay. And the man saw that a long time had passed since it again came to peep (at him); and the thing seemed as if it had altogether gone. And the man thought that he would first wait a little; for, he would (otherwise) startle the lion, if the lion were still at this place. And the man saw that a little time had now passed, and he had not perceived it (the lion); and the thing seemed as if it had really gone away.

And he did nicely at the place yonder where he lay; he did not arise (and) go; for, he arose, be first sprang to a different place, while he wislied that the lion should not know the place to which he seemed to have gone. He, when he had done in this manner, ran in a zigzag direction,[2]

1. The lion, this time when it came back to look at the man, only had its head and shoulders in sight.
2. He did not run straight; but ran first in one direction, then sprang to another place, then rau again, etc.

while he desired that the lion should not smell out his footsteps, that the lion should not know the place to which he seemed to have gone; that the lion, when it came, should come to seek about for him (there). Therefore, he thought that he would run in a zigzag direction, so that the lion might not smell out his footsteps; that he might go home; for, the lion, when it came, would come to seek for him. Therefore, he would not run straight into the house; for, the lion, when it came (and) missed him, would intend to find his footprints, that the lion might, following his spoor, seek for him, that the lion might see whether it could not get hold of him.

Therefore, when he came out at the top of the hill, he called out to the people at home about it, that he had just been "lifted up"[1] while the sun stood high, he had been "lifted up"; therefore, they must look out many hartebeest-skins, that they might roll him up in them; for, he had just been "lifted up", while the sun was high. Therefore, he thought that the lion would,—when it came out from the place to which it had gone,—it would come (and) miss him; it would resolve to seek (and) track him out. Therefore, he wanted the people to roll him up in many hartebeest-skins, so that the Lion should not come (and) get him. For, they were those who knew that the lion is a thing which acts thus to the thing which it has killed, it does not leave it, when it has not eaten it. Therefore, the people must do thus with the hartebeest-skins, the people must roll him up in them; and also (in) mats; these (are)

1. He avoided(?) the name of the lion; therefore, he in this manner told the people about it.

things which the people must roll him up in, (in order) that the lion should not get him.

And the people did so; the people rolled him up in mats,[1] and also (in) hartebeest-skins, which they rolled together with the inats. For, the man was the one who had spoken thus to them about it; therefore it was that they rolled him up in hartebeestskins, while they felt that their hearts' young man (he) was, whom they did not wish the lion to eat. Therefore, they intended to hide hini well, that the lion should not get hold of him. For, a young man whom they did not a little love he was. Therefore, they did not wish the lion to eat him; and they said that they would cover over the young man with the hut's sheltering bushes,[2] so that the lion, when it came, should come seeking about for the young man it should not get hold of the young man, when it came; it should come seeking about for him.

And the people went out to seek for *!kui-sse* [an edible root]; and they dug out *!kui-sse*; and they brought (home) *!kui-sse*, at noon, and they baked[3] *!kui-sse*. And an old Bushman, as he went along getting wood for his wife, in order that his wife might make a fire above the *!kui-sse*,[4] espied the lion, as the lion eanie over (the top of the hill), at the place which the young man had come over. And he told the house folk about it; and he spoke, he said:

1. Many mats.
2. The screen or shelter of the hut. The narrator uses the word *scherm* for it.
3. In a hole in the ground, which has been previously heated, and which is covered over with earth when the has been put into it.
4. *i.e.* on the top of the earth with which the hole had been covered over.

"Ye are those who see the hill yonder, its top, the place yonder (where) that young man came over, what it looks like!"

And the young man's mother spoke, she said:

Ye must not allow the lion to come into the huts;[1] ye must shoot it dead, when it has not (yet) come to the huts."

And the people slung on their quivers; and they went to meet the lion; and they were shooting at the lion; the lion would not die, although the people were shooting at it.

And another old woman spoke, she said: "Ye must give to the lion a child, (in order) that the lion may go away from us." The lion answered, it said that it did not want a child; for, it wanted the person whose eyes' tears it had licked; he was the one whom it wanted.

And the (other) people speaking, said: "In what manner were ye shooting at the lion that ye could not manage to kill the lion?" And another old man spoke, he said: "Can ye not see that (it) must be a sorcerer? It will not die when we are shooting at it; for, it insists upon (having) the man whom it carried off."

The people threw children to the lion; the lion did not want the children which the people threw to it; for, it, looking, left them alone.

The people were shooting[2] at it, while it sought for the man,—that it might get hold of the man,—the people were shooting at it. The people

1. The narrator explains here that several huts, were in a row; the mother means all the huts, not merely one. The lion must not come into the *werf* (= "yard", or "ground").
2. They wanted to shoot him dead, before he could find the man.

said: Ye must bring for us assegais, we must kill[1] the lion." The people were shooting at it; it did not seem as if the people were shooting at it; they were stabbing[2] it with assegais, while they intended to stab it to death. It did not seem as if the people were stabbing it; for, it continued to seek for the young man; it said that it wanted the young man whose tears it had licked; he was the one whom it wanted.

It scratched asunder, breaking to pieces for the people the huts, while it scratched asunder, seeking for the young man. And the people speaking, said: "Can ye not see that the lion will not eat the children whom we have given to it?" And the people speaking, said: "Can ye not see that a sorcerer (it) must be?" And the people speaking, said: "Ye must give a girl to the lion, that we may see whether the lion will not eat her, that it may go away."[3] The lion did not want the girl; for, the lion only wanted the man whom it had carried off; he was the one whom it wanted.

And the people spoke, they said, they did not know in what manner they should act towards the lion; for, it had been morning[4] when they shot at the lion; the lion would not die; for, it had, when the people were shooting at it, it had

1 As their arrows did not seem able to reach a spot which would kill the lion, they thought that they might do better with their assegais.
2. The narrator explains that some threw assegais; others stabbed the lion with them. The people were all round it; but it did not bite them, because it wanted theyoung man whom it had carried off.
3. The lion could not have eaten her at the houses.
4. It was now late, and they had been shooting at the lion since the morning, and did not know what they should now do to get rid of it.

been walking about. "Therefore, we do not know in what manner we shall act towards the lion. For, the children whom we gave to the lion, the lion has refused, on account of the man whom it had carried off."

And the people speaking, said: "Say ye to the young man's mother about it, that she must, although she loves the young man, she must take out the young man, she must give the young man to the lion, even if he be the child of her heart. For, she is the one who sees that the sun is about to set, while the lion is threatening us; the lion will not go (and) leave us; for, it insists upon (having) the young man."

And the young man's mother spoke, she said:

Ye may give my child to the lion; ye shall not allow the lion to eat my child; that the lion may go walking about; for, ye shall killing lay it upon my child; that it may die, like my child; that it may die, lying upon my child."

And the people, when the young man's mother had thus spoken, the people took the young man out from the hartebeest-skins in which they had rolled him up, they gave the young man to the lion. And the lion bit the young man to death; the people, when it was biting at the young man, were shooting at it; the people were stabbing it; and it bit the young man to death.

And the lion spoke, it said to the people about it, that this time was the one at which it would die; for, it had got hold of the man for whom it had been seeking; it had got hold of him!

And it died, while the man also lay dead; it also lay dead, with the man.

A WOMAN OF THE EARLY RACE AND THE RAIN BULL.

The Rain formerly courted(?) a young woman, while the young woman was in (her) hut, because she felt that she was still ill. The Rain scented her, and the Rain went forth, on account of it; while the place became misty.[1] And he, in this manner, courting(?) came, while he courted(?) the young woman on account of her scent. He in this manner trotting came; while the young woman was lying down, while she held (her) child (by her) on the kaross; she was lying down.

And she lay, smelling the Rain's scent, while the place was fragrant,[2] while the place felt that his (the Rain's) breath was that which closed in the place; it was that[3] through which he coming passed; it resernbled a mist.

And the young woman became aware of him, as he came up; while he lowered his tail (?). And the young woman perceived him,[4] as he came past her, at, the side of the hut. And the young woman

1. Resembling a fog (or mist). The people spoke tbus, they said to nue that the Rain's breath was wont to shut in the place, when he came out to seek food; (while) he was eating about, the mist was "sitting" there,
2. The Rain's scent it was. The people say that there is no scent as sweet, hence the people say that it is fragrant.
3. His breath is that through which he passing comes.
4. He resembled a bull, while he felt that (he) was the Rain's body.
5. The word *Xoro* also means an ox; but the narrator explained that a bull (*Xoro gwai*) is meant here.

exclaimed: "Who can this man be who comes to me?" while he, crouching (?)[1], came up.[2]

The young woman took up buchu in her hand, the young woman threw buchu upon his forehead. And she arose; and she pressed (the buchu) down upon his forehead (with her hand); she pushed him away; and she took up (her) kaross; she tied it on.

The young woman took up the child,[3] she held the child very nicely; she, holding (it) very nicely, laid the child down upon a kaross; she, covering (it), laid the child[4] away.

She mounted the Rain; and the Rain took her away.[5] She went along; she went along looking at the trees. And she went along, she spoke, she said: "Thou must go to the tree standing yonder, the one that is big, thou shalt go (and) set me down at it. For I ache; thou shalt first go to

1. His ears (they) were; those which he laid down; while he felt that he crouched (?).
2. While he felt that he stood in front of the opening of the hut.
3. She seems to have laid the child away for (her) husband; while she felt that she was not going to live; for, she would living go, go, go, go, she would go to become a frog, for the Rain intended that she should go to the water pit, that water pit from which he went forth, he courting (?) went.
4. At the hut. She laid it down, while she thought that she should die, (and) go to become a frog.
5. While the Rain felt that the Rain was going to the Rain's home, the pit from which he came out. Therefore, the young woman said he should go to let her sit down.

    The people say that the Rain's Bull goes out from his pit, and the Pit becomes dry, while it feels that the Rain has gone out, the Rain's Bull. Therefore, the pit dries up on account of it.

set me down at it." Therefore, the Rain trotted, taking her straight to the |*kuerriten*|*kuerriten*.[1] And he trotted up to the |*kuerriten*|*kuerriten*. And the young woman said: "Thou must go underneath, close to the stem of the tree." Therefore, he went underneath, close to the stem of the tree. The young woman looked at him; the young woman took out buchu, she rubbed him (with it).[2] Then the Rain went to sleep, on account of it.

Therefore, when she saw that the Rain slept, she climbed up, she stole softly away, she climbed up, she climbed along (?) the |*kuerriten*|*kuerriten*. And she descended at a distance, she in this manner stole softly along, while the Rain continued to sleep. She, afar, softly returned home; while the Rain awoke behind her back, when the Rain felt that the place was becoming cool.

He arose, he walked away; he went away to the middle of the spring(?) from which he had courting(?) gone out, while he believed that the young woman was still sitting upon his back. He went away, he went away to the water. He went into (it), while the young woman went along, she went to burn buchu; while she was "green", while

1. It is a large tree, which is found in kloofs.
2. The singular form of |*kuerriten*|*kuerriten* is, |*hang#kass'o* says, |*kui*|*kuerri*. It is the name of a bush found in the ravines of a 'red' mountain, on this side of Kenhardt, called Rooiberg by the white men. (VIII-21, p. 7835.)
3. Rubbed his neck (with buchu).
4. With dry things they rub. Therefore, they are wont to say that they rub 'with them.
    If things are wet, they are wont to say that they anoint with them.

she smelt strongly[1] of the scent of the ||*khou*; she was rubbing herself, while she rubbed, taking away the smell of the ||*khou* from herself.

The old women who had been out seeking food were those who came to burn horns, while they desired that the smell of the horns should go up, so that the Rain should not be angry with them.[2]

1. To smell strongly.
2. Her own scent it was which resembled (that of) the ||*khou*. The ||*khou* (possibly a fungus?) is a thing belonging to the Rain. Her (the young woman's) intelligence was that with which she acted wisely towards the Rain; hence all the people lived; they would (otherwise) have been killed; all (of them) would have become frogs.

THE GIRL'S STORY; THE FROGS' STORY.

A girl formerly lay ill; she was lying down. She did not eat the food which her mothers[1] gave her. She lay ill.

She killed the children of the Water[2]; they were what she ate. Her mothers did not know that she did thus, (that) she killed the Water's children; (that) they were what she ate; she would not eat what her mothers were giving to her.

Her mother was there. They[3] went out to seek Bushman rice. They[4] spoke, they ordered a

1. That is to say, her mother and the other women.
2. !kweiten ta ||ken has not seen these things herself, but she heard that they were beautiful, and striped like a |habba, i.e. zebra.
3. The Water was as large as a bull, and the Water's children were the size of calves, being the children of great things.
4. All the women, and all the children but one.

child[1] to remain at home. The girl did not know (about) the child. And the old woman said that she must look at the things which her elder sister ate. And they left the child at home t; and they Nvent out to seek food (Bushman rice). They intended (?) that the child should look at the things which her elder sister ate.

The elder sister went out from the house of illness, (and) descended to the spring, as she intended again to kill a Water-child. The (Bushman) child was in the hut,[3] while she (the girl) did not know (about) the child. And she went (and) killed a Water-child, she carried the Water-child home. The (Bushman) child was looking; and she (the girl) boiled the Water-child's flesh; and she ate it; and she lay down; and she again went to lie down, while she (the child) beheld her. And she went to lie down, when she felt that she had finished eating. The child looked at her; and she lay down.

And her mother returned. The child told her mother about it; for her elder sister had gone to kill a handsome thing at the water. And her mother said: "It is a Water-child!" And her mother did not speak about it; she again went out to seek for Bushman rice.

And when she was seeking about for food, the clouds came up. And she spoke, she said: "Something is not right at home; for a whirlwind is bringing (things) to the spring. For something is not going on well at home. Therefore, the whirlwind is taking (things) away to the spring."

1. A little girl, as big as a European child of 11.
2. Literally, "allowed "her to remain there.
3. In her mother's hut.

Because her daughter killed the Water's children, therefore the whirlwind took them away to the spring. Something had not gone well at home, for her daughter had been killing the Water's children. That was why the whirlwind took them away to the spring. Because her daughter killed the Water's children, therefore the whirlwind took them away to the spring; because she had killed the Water's children.

The girl was the one who first went into the spring, and then she became a frog. Her mothers afterwards went into the spring; the whirlwind brought them to it, when she was already in the spring. She was a frog. Her mothers also became frogs; while the whirlwind was that which brought them, when they were on the hunting ground; the whirlwind brought them to the spring, when her daughter was already in the spring. She was a frog. And her mothers afterwards came; the whirlwind was that which brought them to it, when they were on the hunting ground. Meanwhile their daughter was in the spring; she was a frog.

Her father also came to become a frog; for the whirlwind brought her father-when he was yonder on the hunting ground-to the spring, (to) the place where his daughter was. Her father's arrows[1] altogether grew out by the spring; for the great whirlwind had brought them to the spring. He also altogether became a frog; likewise his wife, she also became a frog; while she felt that the whirlwind had brought them to the spring. Their things entered that spring (in which) they were. The

1. All the family and their mats were carried into the spring, by the whirlwind, and all their things.

things entered that spring, because they (the people) were frogs. Therefore it was that their things went into the spring, because they were frogs. The mats[1] (grew) out by the spring, like the arrows; their things grew out[2] by the spring.

1. Mats of which the Bushmen make their huts (made from a thick grass or reed?).
2. These things that grow by the springs belonged to the first Bushmen, who preceded the present race, *!kweiten ta ǁken* says. Her mother told her this.

THE MAN WHO ORDERED HIS WIFE TO CUT OFF HIS EARS.

He[1] formerly wished (his) wife to cut off his ears, for his younger brother's head had surely been skinned[2]; whereas his younger brother's wife had only shaved his younger brother's head.

Therefore, (his) wife cut away his ears; although (his) wife had said that she would not do so; he was the one who insisted (upon it).

Therefore, (his) wife cut off his ears; and he was screaming, on account of his skin, while he himself had been the one who wished the wife to do so; for his younger brother's head had surely been skinned; whereas his younger brother had merely had his head shaved; while (his) wife shaved, removing the old hair.[3]

1. !Xwe-|na-sse-!k'e is the name of the Bushmen who lived first in the land.
2. I am one who does not know his name, because the people were those who did not utter his name to me; for, they were men of the early race; therefore, they did foolish things on account of it.
3. He really thought that the skin of his younger brother's head was off, while it was his younger brother's head's hair which had been shaved away.

THE #NERRU AND HER HUSBAND.[1]

A man of the early race formerly married a *#nerru*.[2] The *#nerru* put[3] the dusty (ie. earthy) Bushman rice into a bag, when her husband had dug out (literally, "had killed") Bushman rice. She went to wash the Bushman rice; they returned home.

They early went out to seek for food on the morrow, she and (her) husband; for she was alone(?) with her husband. He was the one who dug[4] out (Bushman rice). Therefore she was with her husband. Thus she went out to seek for food, on the morrow. The husband dug out Bushman rice; he put the Bushman rice into the bag.[5] And the husband again dug out other Bushman rice. He put it in above, put in the Bushman rice on the top of the morning's Bushman rice. He again arose, he sought for other Bushman rice. He again found other Bushman rice; he dug out

1. think that |*Xabbi-ang*'s grandmother's grandmother's other grandmother's mother it must have been who formerly, in this manner, spoke to her.
2. The *#nerru* (now a bird) was formerly a person; therefore, a man of the early race was the one who married her.
3. When they are putting Bushman rice into (a bag), when the Bushman rice has earth with it, they say that they *!ko* Bushman rice.
4. "To dig with a stick" is here meant.
5. The man was the one who was putting Bushman rice into the bag, while the woman was the one who was holding the bag; she was the one who intended to shake in the Bushman rice. He stood inside the mouth of the hole, while the wife stood above.

(the earth from it). And he again dug it (the rice) out. He put it on the top (of the other). He put it on the top; and the bag[1] became full.

And he arose, he sought for other Bushman rice. He found other Bushman rice; he dug but (the earth from) it. He dug it out. And he exclaimed: "Give me (thy) little kaross,[2] that I may put the Bushman rice upon it." And the wife said:[3] "We are not accustomed to put Bushman rice, having earth with it, into our back's kaxoss, we who are of the house of #*nerru*."[4] And he exclaimed: "Give me, give me the little kaross, that I may put the Bushman rice upon (it)." And the wife said: "Thou shouldst put the Bushman rice into the ground; for we are not accustomed to put Bushman rice, having earth with it, into our back's kaross." And he exclaimed: "Give me, give me the little kaross, that I may put the Bushman rice upon (it)." And the wife exclaimed: "Thou shouldst put the Bushman rice into the ground, that thou mayst cover over the Bushman rice."[5]

And he exclaimed: "Give me the kaross, that I may put the Bushman rice upon (it)!" while he snatched away the kaross. The wife's entrails,

1. I think that it seems to have been a springbok sack (i.e. a bag made of springbok skin).
2. It is a little kaross. One skin (that is, the skin of one animal) they call *!koussi*.
3. She spoke gently (i.e. did not sing here).
4. I think that their houses must have been numerous; for they were numerous; for, when they are little birds, they are not a little numerous.
5. With other earth.

which were upon the little kaross,[1] poured down.[2] And he, crying, exclaimed: "Oh dear! O my wife! What shall I do? "while the wife arose, the wife said (*i.e.* sang)-

> "We, who are of the house of #*nerru*,
> We are not used to put earthy Bushman rice
> (Into) our back's kaross;
> We, who are of the house of #*nerru*,
> We are not used to put earthy Bushman rice
> (Into) our back's kaross:"

while she walked on replacing her entrails. She sang-[3]

> "We, who are of the house of #*nerru*,
> We are not used to put earthy Bushman rice
> (Into) our back's kaross:"

Therefore, her mother, when sitting,[4] exclaimed: "Look at the place to which (thy) elder sister went to seek food, for the noise of the wind is that which sounds like a person; "for, (thy) elder sisters' husbands do not act rightly. Thou dost see that the noise of the wind is that which sounds like a person, singing to windward." And her daughter stood up; her daughter looked. She (the daughter) exclaimed: "(Thy) daughter is the one who falling comes." Then her mother said: "I wish that ye may see; (thy) elder sisters' husbands[6] do

1. I do not know well (about it), for my people were those who spoke thus; they said that the #*nerru*'s entrails were formerly upon the little kaross.
2. She was sitting down.
3. She went along singing, as she went away home (to her mother's home).
4. She was sitting at home.
5. Her daughter was the one of whom she spoke, (of) her singing.
6. I think that she was speaking of her daughter's husband.

mad things, as if they do not seem to understand; they marry among us (literally, 'into us') as if they understood."

Then she ran to meet her daughter; she went to put the little kaross[1] upon her daughter; she, holding, put her daughter's entrails upon the little kaross; and she bound up her daughter;[2] she slowly conducted her daughter home; she went to take her daughter into her (the mother's) hut.

Therefore, she was angry about her daughter; when her daughter's husband wanted to come to his wife, she was angry. Therefore, her daughter's husband went back to his own people, when she had said that her daughter's husband should go back; for, they did not understand. Therefore, her daughter's husband went back; while they[3] continued to dwell (there).

1. Her mother's new little kaross, which had been unused (lit. "sitting"), and which she had put away.
2. With the four straps of the !*k'oussi*, formed by the four legs of the springbok's skin
3. i.e., the #*nerru*, many #*nerru*.

THE #NERRU, AS A BIRD

The *#nerru*'s bill is very short. The male *#nerru* is the one whose plumage resembles (that of) the ostrich; it is black like the male ostrich. The female *#nerru* is the one whose plumage is white like (that of) the female ostrich. Thus, they resemble the ostriches; because the male *#nerru* are black, the female *#nerru* white.

They eat the things which little birds usually eat, which they pick up on the ground.

They make grass nests on the ground, by the root of a bush.

When not breeding, they are found in large numbers.

THE DEATH OF THE LIZARD.

The Lizard[1] formerly sang—

> "For,
> I therefore intend to go,
> Passing through,
> !guru-|na's pass.

> "And,
> I therefore intend to go,
> Passing through,
> |Xe-!khwai's pass.

> For,
> I therefore intend to go,
> passing through,
> !guru-|na's pass,

> "For,
> I therefore intend to go,
> Passing through,
> |Xe-!khwai's pass.

And, when he was passing through, the mountains[2] squeezing broke him, when he had intended to pass through; for, he seems to have thought that he would spring through the mountain pass, which was like this (the narrator here showed

1. The !khau was a man of the early race. He is now a lizard of the genus *Agama*. "Chiefly found in rocky and sandy places. Many species distributed all through South Africa."
2. These mountains are large ones, near |itten|hing.

the first and second fingers of his left hand in a forked and almost upright position). Then, the mountains caught him thus (putting his fingers close together), the mountains bit, breaking him. Therefore, his forepart fell over[1] (and) stood still) it became *!guru-|na*; while his hinder part fell over (and) stood still; it was that which became *|Xe-!khwai*.

REMARKS ON THE PRECEDING STORY BY THE NARRATOR.

I think that he seems to have been going to the red sand hills, that he might come (and) dwell at them. For, I think that the (shallow) pools, which lie among the red sand hills, seem to have been those towards which he was going, that he might come (and) live at them. He seems to have been going towards *!kaugen-|ka|ka* (a certain pool), that he might come (and) live at it. For, I think that *!kaugen-|ka|ka* is near this place. He is the one who, when he came passing through, would come along the 'vlei', that he might ascend, passing along the side of the hill; and he would altogether descend into *||na-||kuarra* (a certain river), and he would go quite down, along (the river bed) to *!kaugen-|ka|ka*. *!kaugen-|ka|ka* would be the place where he descended; it was where he was going to dwell; it must, I think, be the place towards which he appears to have been going. He broke (in twain) when he seems to have been going towards it.

1. It verily (?) turning over went.

VI. POETRY.

THE CAT'S SONG.

    Ha¹ ha ha,
    Ha, Ha,

I am the one whom the Lynx derides,
I am the one who did not run fast;
For, the Lynx is the one who runs fast,

    Ha¹ ha ha,
    Ha, Ha,

I am the one whom the Lynx derides.

    Ya Ya Ya,
    Ya Ya,

I am the one whom the Lynx derides.
I am the one who could not run fast,

    Ya Ya Ya,
    Ya Ya,

I am the one whom the Lynx derides,
"The Cat could not run fast."

    Ya Ya Ya,
    Ya Ya,

The Cat is the one whom the Lynx derides,
"It is the one who could not run fast,"

> Ya Ya Ya,
> Ya Ya,

The Cat is the one who could not run fast,
It was not cunning.

<small>1. Here the cat opens its mouth wide in singing.</small>

It did foolish things;
For, the Lynx is one who understands,
The Cat does not understand."
The Cat (nevertheless) is cunning.

> Ya Ya Ya,
> Ya Ya,

The Cat is the one about whom the Lynx talked.
"It is the one who could not run fast."
It had to be cunning.[1]
For, the Lynx is one who is cunning.

> Haggla[2] haggla haggla
> haggla haggla
> Heggle heggle heggle
> heggle heggle
> Heggli heggli heggli
> Heggli ng!

1. Reference is here made to the Cat's way of doubling when pursued.
2. The narrator here explains that the Cat "talks with its tongue", assenting to what it has been saying.

THE SONG OF THE CAAMA FOX.

Crosser of the Spoor, Crosser of the Spoor,[1]
Crosser of the Spoor, Crosser of the Spoor!

1. The Caama Fox is called "Crosser of the Spoor", because it avoids the dog nicely when the dog chases it, and, turning suddenly, runs back, crossing the dog's spoor (behind it), while the dog is racing on in front, thinking to catch the Caama Fox by so doing.

Cross the Caama Fox's spoor,
Cross the Caama Fox's spoor![1]

Cross the Caama Fox's spoor,
Cross the Caama Fox's spoor!

1. It sings that the dog appears to think that he will kill it; but the dog will not kill it; for it is the one who crosses the spoor of (another) Caamaa Fox. It is the one which that dog will not kill; for the dog is the one who will nearly(?) die of fatigue, when it (the Caama Fox) has gone to lie peacefully in the shade; while it does not feel tired; while the dog painfully goes back to his master.

THE SONGS OF THE BLUE CRANE.

1. It is the Blue Crane's story which it sings; it sings (about) its shoulder, namely, that the "krieboom" berries are upon its shoulder; it goes along singing—

> The berries are upon my shoulder,
> The berries are upon my shoulder,
> The berry it[1] is upon my shoulder,

1. Its name is one; they (the berries) are numerous; its name is (still) one. The "krieboom" berries are many; the name of the berries is one. It appears as if its berry were one, (but) they are many.

    The word |gara is the same in the singular and plural, viz., |gara (or |gara tsaXau) a !kwai, "one |gara berry," and |gara (or |gara tsaXaiten) e |Ukwaiya, "many |gara berries." The |gara is a part of the ||na, or "krieboom", the berries of it, as far as I can understand. They are said to be round, white, and "hard" (i.e., they have something hard inside them). The outside flesh is sweet. They are eaten by the Koranna and the Bushmen. The women go to the "krieboom", pick the berries, put them into a bag and take them home to eat, first mixing them with other berries. They do not eat them unmixed, on account of their teeth, as they fear that the sweetness of the berries might otherwise render their teeth unfit to chew meat well.

> The berries are upon my shoulder.
> The berries are up here (on its shoulder),[1]
> *Rrru* are up here;
> The berries are up here,
> *Rrru* are up here,
> Are up here;
> The berries *Rrru* are put away (upon) it (its shoulder)."

2.

(When running away from a man.)

A splinter of stone which is white,[2]
A splinter of stone which is white,
A splinter of stone which is white.

3.

(When walking slowly, leaving the place [walk of peace].)

A white stone splinter,
A white stone splinter.

4.

(When it flaps its wings.)

Scrape (the springbok skin[3] for) the bed.
Scrape (the springbok skin for) the bed.

Rrrru rrra,
Rrru rrra
Rru rra!

1. ||*kabbo* cannot explain why the berries do not roll off; he says that he does not know. This is a song of the very old people, the "first" old people, which was in his thoughts.
2. ||*kabbo* explains that the bird sings about its head, which is something of the shape of a stone knife or splinter, and has white feathers. He says that Bushmen, when without a knife, use a stone knife for cutting up game. They break a stone, knocking off a flat splinter from it, and cut up the game with that. The Grass Bushmen, ||*kabbo* says, make arrowheads of white quartz points (crystal points, as far as could be understood).
3. The Bushmen make beds (*i.e.*, skins to sleep on) from the skins of springbok and goats.

THE OLD WOMAN'S SONG.

First Version.

The old Woman sings; goes singing along; sings as she goes; the old Woman sings as she goes along about the Hyena-

"The old she Hyena,
The old she Hyena,

Was carrying off the old Woman from the old hut;

The old Woman in this manner,
She sprang aside,
She arose,
She beat the Hyena.
The Hyena, herself,
The Hyena killed[1] the Hyena."

Second Version.

The old she Hyena,
The old she Hyena,
Was carrying off the old Woman,
As the old Woman lay in the old hut.[2]

---

1. She killed herself, by casting herself violently upon the pointed rock on which she had intended to cast the old Woman who was upon her back; but the old Woman sprang aside and saved herself.
2. The old Woman, who was unable to walk, lay in an old, deserted hut. Before her sons left her, they had closed the circle [sides] of the hut, as well as the door-opening, with sticks from the other huts, leaving the top of the hut open, so that she should feel the sun's warmth. They had left a fire for her, and had fetched more dry wood. They were obliged to leave her behind, as they were all starving, and she was too weak to go with them to seek food at some other place.

A SONG SUNG BY THE STAR !GAUNU, AND ESPECIALLY BY BUSHMAN WOMEN.

Does the ||*garraken*[1] flower open?
The #*ku-Yam*[2] is the one which opens.
Dost thou open?
The #*ku-Yam* is the one which opens.

1. The ||*garraken* are bulbs; the Bushmen dig them out.
2. *Dimorphotheca annua*, a daisy-like flower, in bloom at Mowbray in August, 1879.

SIRIUS AND CANOPUS.

My (step)grandmother, *Ttuai-ang*, was the one who used to rejoice about Canopus. She said—

>Sirius!
>Sirius!
>Winks like
>Canopus!
>
>Canopus
>Winks like
>Sirius!
>
>Canopus
>Winks like
>Sirius!
>
>Sirius
>Winks like
>Canopus!

While my grandmother felt that food was abundant.[1]

1. We are wont to say *!Xu*, when food is abundant.

THE SONG OF THE BUSTARD.

My younger brother-in-law,
Put my head in the fire.[1]
My younger brother-in-law,
My younger brother-in-law,
Put my head in the fire.

When we startle it up, it flies away; it (cries): "*Wara ǁkhau, wara ǁkhau, wara ǁkhau, ǁkhau ǁkhau, ǁkhau, wara ǁkhau, wara ǁkhau, wara ǁkhau, ǁkhau ǁkhau, ǁkhau!*"

When it stands on the ground, it says: "*A wa, a wa, a wa, a wa!*" when it stands on the ground.

1. When the "Knorhaan Brandkop" was still a man, his head was thrust into the fire by his brother-in-law, in order to punish him for having surreptitiously married a sister. Since then he is only a bustard.

THE SONG OF THE SPRINGBOK MOTHERS.

The Springbok mothers sang (soothing their children)—

> "A-a' hng
> O Springbok Child!
> sleep for me.
> A-a' hng
> O Springbok Child!
> Sleep for me."

||KABBO'S SONG ON THE LOSS OF HIS TOBACCO POUCH.[1]

Famine it is,
Famine it is,
Famine is here.

Famine it is,
Famine it is,
Famine is here.

Famine ["tobacco-hunger" is meant here]-he did not smoke, because a dog had come in the

1. It was stolen by a hungry dog, named "Blom ", which belonged to !gou!nui.

night (and) carried off from him his pouch. And he arose in the night, he missed his pouch. And then he again lay down, while he did not smoke. And we were early seeking for the pouch. We did not find the pouch.

THE BROKEN STRING.

People were those who
Broke for me the string.
Therefore,
The place became like this to me,
On account of it,
Because the string was that which broke for me.[1]
Therefore,
The place does not feel to me,
As the place used to feel to me,
On account of it.
For,
The place feels as if it stood open before me,
Because the string has broken for me.
Therefore,
The place does not feel pleasant to me,
On account of it.

The above is a lament, sung by *Xaa-tting* after the death of his friend, the magician and rain-maker *!nuing|kui-ten*, who died from the effects of a shot he received when going about, by night, in the form of a lion.

1. Now that "the string is broken", the former "ringing sound in the sky" is no longer heard by the singer, as it had been in the magician's lifetime.

THE SONG OF !NU!NUMMA-!KWITEN.

!nu!numma-!kwiten[1] formerly said (sang)-

> "Hng-ng, hng;
> I kill children who cry;
> Hng-ng, hng.
> I kill children who cry;
> Hng-ng, hng;
> I kill children who cry.

A beast of prey (he, *!nu!numma-!kwiten*) is. My grandfather used to say (that) *!nu!numma-!kwiten* formerly said-

> "Hng-ng, hng;
> I kill children who cry;
> "Hng-ng, hng;
> I kill children who cry;

When my grandfather wished that we should leave off making a noise,[2] he said that *!nu!numma-!kwiten* formerly used to say

> "Hng-ng, hng;
> I kill children who cry;
> "Hng-ng, hng;
> I kill children who cry;

---

1. The narrator gave the following explanation of *!nu!numma-!kwiten*'s name:—

    "A man who eats great (pieces of) meat, he cuts them off, he puts them into his mouth. I think that eggs are white; therefore, I think that his name seems to be 'White-Mouth'."

    "*!nu!numma-!kwiten* is a beast of prey. A man was the one who gobbled eggs, swallowed down eggs. Therefore, be was [his name was] *!kotta-kkoe*." Reference is

135

here made to a man of the early race, who swallowed ostrich eggs whole, and is the chief figure in a legend related by |han#kass'o (V.—56. L.).

2. We were calling out, making a noise there, as we played.

And (when) he hears a little child crying there, he follows the sound to it, while the little child is crying there, he, following the sound, goes to it, approaches it stealthily, approaching stealthily, reaches the hut, in which the little child is crying. He springs, springs into the hut. He catches hold of the little child) he springs, taking it away. He goes to swallow it down. He departs.

B. HISTORY (NATURAL AND PERSONAL).

VII. ANIMALS AND THEIR HABITS-ADVENTURES WITH THEM-AND HUNTING.

THE LEOPARD AND THE JACKAL.

The jackal watches the leopard, when the leopard has killed a springbok. The jackal whines (with uplifted tongue), he begs the leopard for springbok flesh. He howls, he begs, for he is a jackal. Thus he howls, he indeed begs, because he is a jackal. Therefore he howls when he begs, he indeed wants the leopard to give him flesh, that he may eat, that he also may eat.

Then the leopard is angry, the leopard kills him, the leopard bites him dead, he lifts him up, he goes to put him into the bushes; thus he hides him.

DOINGS OF THE SPRINGBOK.

The mother springbok is wont to do thus, as she trots along, when she has a springbok kid which is little, she grunts,[1] as she trots along; she says—"*a, a, a*"[2] as she trots along. Therefore they (the springbok) make a resounding noise(?), because they are numerous; while the springbok kids also cry (bleat), while their mothers cry (grunt). Their mothers say—"*a, a, a*," the springbok kids say-

1. Because she protectingly takes along the child, she grunts, as the child plays.
2. Here the narrator made a grunting noise which, he said, was "in his throat"; and about which he remarked—"When I sit imitating the springbok, then I cough, on account of it."

"*me, me, me*," while their mothers say "*a, a, a*," as they grunt. The springbok children say "*me, me, me*," while their mothers say "*a, a, a*," as they grunting go forward.

Therefore,[1] we are wont to say—"O beast of prey! thou art the one who hearest the place behind, it is resonant with sound. Therefore, I said that I would sit here. For these male springbok which stand around, are those which will go along, passing behind you; because I am lying down, and they do not perceive me; they will have to (?) go along, passing behind you, when ye have gone behind (the hill); they will have to (?) go along, passing behind you."

1. Therefore, the Bushmen are wont to say: "O beast of prey! it (the herd of springbok) seems as if it will arise; for thou art the one who seest the springbok's children. For thou art the one who seest (that) the springbok's children seem as if (they) would arise." (They had been lying down, or, as the narrator expressed it, "sitting.")

HABITS OF THE BAT AND THE PORCUPINE.

Mamma said to me that the bat,[1] when the porcupine is still at the place where it is seeking about for food, does not come, for the bat remains with it, while it is seeking about for food, When it (the porcupine) returns home, then it is that the bat comes to its hole;[2] then I know that the porcupine appears to have returned.

1. The bat's other name is !|gogen.
2. The bat inhabits the same hole as the porcupine.

Mamma told me about it, that I should watch for the porcupine, if I saw the bat; then I know, that the porcupine appears to come; for the bat comes. And I must not sleep; for I must watch for the porcupine; for, when the porcupine approaches, I feel sleepy, I become sleepy (on account of) the porcupine; for the porcupine is a thing which is used, when it draws near, to go along making us sleep against our will, as it wishes that we may not know the time at which it comes; as it wishes that it may come into the hole while we are asleep. Therefore, it goes along making us sleep; while it wishes that it may come, while we are asleep, that it may smell whether harm awaits it at the hole, whether a man is lying in wait for it at the hole. And if the man is asleep it steals softly away [lifting its quills that they may not rattle], when it has smelt the man's scent. Therefore it is used to cause us to become sleepy, when it wishes to smell whether peace it be.

Therefore mamma used to tell me that I should do thus, even if I felt sleepy, I should know that the porcupine was the one who went along making me sleepy against my will; it was the one who went along causing me to sleep. I should do thus, even if I felt that I wanted to sleep, I should not sleep; for the porcupine would come, if I slept there. And the porcupine would steal gently away, while I slept. I should not know the time at which the porcupine came; I should think that the porcupine had not come, while the porcupine bad long come; it had come (and) gone away, while I slept. Therefore, I should not sleep, that I might know when the porcupine came. For, I should do thus, if I slept, I should not know when it came.

Therefore, I am used to do thus, when I lie in wait for a porcupine, I do not sleep, when 1 am watching for the porcupine; the porcupine comes, while I am watching for it; I see it return, while I feel that I am the one who did not sleep. For mamma was the one who thus told me, that I must not sleep, even if I felt sleepy; I must do as father used to do, when father watched well for the porcupine. Therefore, father used to know when the porcupine came, while he felt that he watched for the porcupine. Therefore, he used to know when the porcupine came; even if he felt sleepy, he did not sleep, because he felt that he wanted to know the time at which theporcupine came.

For, these things are those about which my mother and the others told me, namely, did I not see that the porcupine is a thing which does not go (about) at noon; for it goes (about) by night; for it cannot see at noon. Therefore, it goes (about) by night, while it feels that night is (the time) at which it sees; it would, if it went (about) at noon, it would be going into the bushes, while it felt that its eyes were not comfortable. Therefore, it would be going into the bushes, while it felt that its eyes were not comfortable. For its eyes would feel dazzled. Night is (the time) when it sees well. For, it knows that this is the time, at which it perceives; on the place where it goes it sees the bushes at night.

Father used to tell me that, when lying in wait for a porcupine, at the time at which the Milky Way turns back, I should know that it is the time at which the porcupine returns. Father taught me about the stars; that I should do thus when lying in wait at a porcupine's hole, I must watch the stars; the place where the stars fall,[1] it is the one which I must thoroughly watch. For this place it really is which the porcupine is at, where the stars fall.

I must also be feeling (trying) the wind. Things which I should watch, father in this manner taught me about, things which I should watch. Father said to me about it, that I should not watch the wind (i.e. to windward), for the porcupine is not a thing which will return coming right out of the wind. For, it is used to return crossing the wind in a slanting direction, because it wants to smell. Therefore, it goes across the wind in a slanting direction, because it wants to smell; for its nostrils are those which tell it about it, whether harm is at this place.

Father used to tell me, that I must not breathe strongly when lying in wait for a porcupine; for, a thing which does not a little hear,[2] it is. I should also not rustle strongly; for, a porcupine is a thing which does not a little hear. Therefore, we are used gently to turn ourselves when sitting; because we fear that had we done so (noisily), as it came, it would have heard.[3]

1. The porcupine will come from the place at which the star seemed to fall.
2. A thing whose ears hear finely it indeed(?) is. Therefore, we do not rustle much on account of it; because (it is) a thing which, even if we thought that we had not rustled much, would hear.
3. If the porcupine had heard, it would have turned back.

THE SAXICOLA CASTOR[1] AND THE WILD CAT.

It (the Saxicola Castor) says: "*Tcha, tcha, tcha, tcha,*" when it is laughing at the wild cat, when it has espied the cat, while the cat is lying down, lying asleep; and it is laughing at the cat, on account of it.

The other little birds (hearing it) go to it, they are all laughing at the cat.

1. The |*ka-kau* or *Saxicola Castor* is a little bird found in Bushmanland. It lives in trees and flies about. It is not eaten by Bushmen.

THE BABOONS AND
||XABBITEN||XABBITEN.

The baboons espied ||*Xabbiten*||*Xabbiten.* as he was coming away from the white men whom he had been to visit. He was carrying flonr, which the white men gave him. And the baboons said: "Uncle ||*Xabbiten*||*Xabbiten* seems to be returning yonder; let us cross his path (?), that we may knock him down."

The baboons did so; ||*Xabbiten*||*Xabbiten* thought he would speak to them, he asked them what they were saying. And ||*Xabbiten*||*Xabbiten* remarked upon their foreheads' steepness (?).[1] And the baboons angrily came down to ||*Xabbiten*||*Xabbiten*; they

---

1. "Ye speak to me! ye are ugly! your foreheads resemble overhanging cliffs!" The baboons became angry with him, because he derided them; he said that their foreheads resembled overhanging cliffs. And they broke off sticks, on account of it they went towards ||*Xabbiten*||*Xabbiten.*

---

broke off sticks, with which they intended to come to beat ||*Xabbiten*||*Xabbiten.*

The baboons' children also came; going along, they called out to their parents.about it: "O fathers! ye must give us ||*Xabbiten*||*Xabbiten*'s head that we may play with it."

||*Xabbiten*||*Xabbiten* did as follows, when he heard that the baboons' children were speaking in this manner, he thought to himself, 'What shall I do? for the baboons are not a little numerous.' He thought, If will climb a krieboom, that I may sit above in the krieboom; the baboons will have (?) to drag me down from the krieboom.'

And the baboons went up to him, as he sat above in the krieboom; the baboons' children spoke to each other about it, they said: "First look ye at ||*Xabbiten*||*Xabbiten*'s big head; we should be a long while playing there, with ||*Xabbiten*||*Xabbiten*'s head; for ye are those who see that its bigness is like this; it seems as if it would not quickly break. "A baboon, who was grown up,[1] spoke to the baboons' children; he questioned the baboons' children: Did not the baboons' children see that ||*Xabbiten*||*Xabbiten* was grown up-that they who were children should think that they could possess the pieces of ||*Xabbiten*||*Xabbiten*. They spoke as if he were their little cousin; that they should possess his pieces. Did they not see that those who are grown up would be the ones to get the pieces of ||*Xabbiten*||*Xabbiten* those who are grown up?

And ||*Xabbiten*||*Xabbiten* thought to himself: 'What shall I do, (in order) that the baboons may

1. The name of the head baboon, the big, old one, which goes after the rest, is *!ubai|ho|kwa*, or "Schildwacht"

leave me? for, they speak angrily about me. it sounds as if they would really attack me.' And 11 e ||*Xabbiten*||*Xabbiten* thought to himself: 'Wait, I will first tell about the baboons to the white men. For baboons are not a little afraid of a gun; I shall see whether they will not be afraid, if they hear that I am talking about them to the white men.'

And ||*Xabbiten*||*Xabbiten* called out,—while he deceived them,-he said: "O white men! the baboons are here, they are with me, ye must drive them away"(?). And the baboons did thus, when they heard that ||*Xabbiten*||*Xabbiten* spoke about them, that the white men should drive them away (?), the baboons looked about, on account of it. And the baboons ran, leaving ||*Xabbiten*||*Xabbiten*; and he escaped, at the time when the baboons went away in fear, he quickly descended from the krieboom. He ran away, as he escaped from the baboons; while they ran to the cliffs he ran away.

A LION'S STORY.

The child cried there for "Bushman rice"; a lion hearing came to her, while she cried there; her parents lay asleep; she sat by them, sat crying.

And the lion heard, as she cried there, And the lion came to her, on account of it.

And she took out (some of) the grass[1] upon which her parents were lying; because she had perceived the lion; the lion intended to kill (and) carry

1. The narrator explained that the Bushmen sleep upon grass, which, in course of time, becomes dry.

off her parents; she set the lion on fire with it;[1] the lion ran away; the bushes took fire.[2] Because the child had set the lion on fire.

And the child's mother afterwards gave her "Bushman rice" (because) she felt that the lion would have killed them) if the child had not set the lion on fire with grass.

And the lion went to die on account of the fire. Because the fire had burned, killing it.

And the child's mother said: "Yes, my child, hadst thou not in this manner set the lion on fire we should have died. For thou didst set the lion on fire for us, for we should have died, hadst thou not set the lion on fire for us. Therefore it is, that we will break for thee an ostrich eggshell of "Bushman rice"; for, thou hast made us to live; we should have been dead, we should have died, hadst thou not set the lion on fire for us; hadst thou not, in this manner, set the lion on fire for us, we should have died."

1. She set the lion's hair on fire.
2. As he ran through the bushes, they caught fire also.

THE MAN WHO FOUND
A LION IN A CAVE.

My grandfather, *!Xugen-ddi*, formerly told me, that a man long ago did thus: when the rain fell he thought that he would go (and) sleep in a cave; when a lion had been the one who had made rain for him, so that he should not know the place at which (his) home seemed to be, that he might pass (it) by (in the darkness), so that he might go to a different place, that the lion might get hold of him.

The place was not a little dark, for, he continued to go into the bushes; he did not see the place along which he was walking. He did not know the place at which (his) home seemed to be. And he thought, 'I must go along in the dark-ness seeking for a cave, that I may go to sleep in it, if I find it; I can afterwards in the morning return home; for, the rain does not a little fall upon me.'

And the lion had come first to the cave; it came to wait for the man in the cave.

And it felt that it was also wet; when it had sat (for a little while) inside the cave,. it became warm, and it slept, when it had become warm; while it had thought that it would sit watching for the man, that it might do thus, if the man came in; while the man thought he would look for a place where he could lay down his things; it might catch hold of the man. It had thought so; (but) it fell fast asleep.

And the man came, while it sat asleep. And the man, when he had entered the cave, heard a thing which seemed to breathe; and the man thought: 'Can people have come to the cave? Do they wait at the cave, those who breathe here?' And he thought, 'How is it that the people do not talk, if people (they) be? Can the people have fallen fast asleep, that the people do not speak to me?' And he thought: 'I will not call out to the people, for I do not know, whether they are people; for, 1 will first feel gently about (with my hands), that I may feel whether real people (they) be. For, I should, if it were a different thing, I should call awakening it.'

And he felt about; and he felt that a thing which seemed to have hair was there. And he gently approached a little nearer to it; and he felt well about, and he felt that a lion was the one which slept sitting inside the cave. And he gently stepped backwards (and) turned round; and he went out on tiptoe.

And, when he had gone to a little distance, he ran swiftly, because he thought that the lion would smell his scent (where) he had gone to feel about for the lion; the lion would run to seek him.

And when he had gone to a little distance, when a little time had passed, he heard the lion, because the lion had smelt his scent, while the lion slept. And as the lion had in this manner sat sleeping, the man's scent had entered its nose, and, because of the man's scent, which seemed as if the man were standing beside it, it had growling arisen; because the man's scent which it smelt, seemed as if the man were standing beside it; that was why it snatched,it the place at which the man seemed to be.

And the man heard it; and tlie man exclaimed: "It sounds as if it had perceived my scent; for thou (addressing himself) art the one who hearest that the cave sounds thus; for the lion sounds as if (it) had been startled awake by my scent; for it sounds as if (it) were biting about, seeking[1] for me in the cave." And the man thought, that he would not go home; for, he would run to a different place; for, he knew that the lion would find his spoor; he would afterwards do as follows, when the day

1. The narrator explained that the lion was smelling and growling about, in order to find the person (or persons) whom it had smelt.

had broken)—if the lion had not killed him, he would afterwards look seeking for (his) home in the morning.

And the day broke, while the man was (still) running, because he had heard the lion, namely, the noise that the lion made, while the lion sought to get him. And, as he ran along, he espied the fire of some other people, which they kindled to warm themselves. And he thought: 'I will run to the fire which stands yonder(?), that

149

I may go to the people who are making fire there, that I may go to sleep (among) them.' And he thought: I Dost thou not think (that) our fathers also said to me, that the lion's eye can also sometimes resemble a fire by night? I will look whether it be a real fire which burns there.' And he ran nearer to the fire; he looked, and he saw that people were lying round(?) in front of the fire. And he thought: 'I will go to the people; for the thing seems as if they are people.'

And he went to the people. And he told the people about it: "Do ye think, that I have not walked into death this night? It happened to me that the lion slept; therefore ye see me! For, ye would not have seen me, had the lion not slept; because it slept, hence it is that the thing seems that ye see me; I have come to you. For, I had thought that I would go to wait there (in) the cave, but, the lion had come to wait for me in the cave. I did not know that the lion was sitting inside the cave; I thought that I would feel about, seeking for a place which was dry, that I might lay down my things there. Then, when I walked into the cave, I heard a thing which sounded as if it breathed; and I thought that people seemed also to be waiting there (in) the cave. I heard that the breathing of the thing did not sound like a man; I thought that I would first feel about, while I did not lay down my things. I felt about, while I (still) had my things; and I felt gently about. I felt that I was touching hair; and I became aware that (it) must be a lion which slept, sitting in (the cave). I turned softly back, when I became aware that it was a lion."

He told the other people about it: Did not the other people hear its seeking? Therefore, the other people must watch for the lion; for the lion would come, when the lion had found his spoor. And they heard the lion, as the lion questioned, seeking to get him. The lion asked, where was the man who had come to it—becanse it smelt that the scent of the man's spoor had ceased at this house? The thing seemed, as if he were at this house; it wanted the man to become visible, that it might get hold of the man.

Day broke, while the lion was (still) threatening them. When the day broke, then it was, that the lion went away, leaving the people; because the sun was rising; therefore, it went away, leaving the people, while it felt that the sun rose. For (otherwise), the people would perceive it; for the lion is a thing which is not willing to come to us, when the sun. stands (in the sky).

CERTAIN HUNTING OBSERVANCES, CALLED !NANNA-SSE.

When we show respect to the game, we act in this manner; because we wish that the game may die. For the game would not die if we did not show respect to it.

We do as follows: a thing which does not run fast is that which we eat, when we have shot game; because we desire that the game should also do as it does. For the game is used to do thus, if we eat the flesh of a thing which is fleet, the thing (i.e. the game) arises; it does like that thing of whose flesh we did eat. The thing, also acts like that thing the flesh of which we had eaten, (doing) that which it does.

Therefore, the old people are accustomed to give us the flesh of a thing which is not fleet. They do not give us all (kinds of) food; for they only give us food (of) which they know that it will strengthen the poison, that the poison may kill the game.

The people do thus, when we have shot a gemsbok, they do not give us springbok flesh, for they feel that the springobok does not a little go. For it is used to act thus, even if it be night, it is used to walk about; day breaks, while it is (still) walking about. Therefore the old people do not give us springbok meat; while they feel that the game, if we ate springbok meat, would also do like the springbok; it would not go to a place near at hand, while it felt that we ate springbok which does not sleep, even though it be night. It (the game) would also do that which the springbok does; and the springbok is wont to do thus, when the sun has set for it in one place, the sun arises for it in a different place, while it feels that it has not slept. For it was walking about in the night. Therefore, the old people fear to give us springbok's meat, because they feel that the gemsbok would not be willing to go to sleep, even at night. For it would, travelling in the darkness, let the day break, while it did not sleep.

Therefore, the old people also do not allow us to take hold of springbok's meat with our hands, because our hands, with which we hold the bow, and the arrows, are those with which we are taking hold of the thing's flesh; we shot the thing, and our hands also are as if we had smelt the springbok's scent; because our hands are those which held the arrows (when) we shot the thing. Therefore, if we take hold of springbok's meat, the thing is as if we ate springbok's meat, because our hands are those which (make) the thing seem as if we had eaten springbok's meat with them. We have not eaten springbok's meat; for it is our hands. We think, 'How can it be? I have not smelt the things which I am (now) smelling?' Another man, who is clever, he thus speaks: "Thou must have taken hold of springbok's flesh, it must be that which has acted in this manner; for, I feel that thou dost not seem to have smelt other things."

Therefore, the people are used to act thus with regard to the man who shot the thing, they do not allow him to carry the springbok; they let him sit down at a little distance, while he is not near to the place where the people are cutting up the springbok. For he sits at a little distance, because he fears lest he should smell the scent of the springbok's viscera(?); that is why he sits at a little. distance, because he wishes that he may not smell the scent of the springbok's viscera

!NANNA-SSE SECOND PART.

FURTHER INFORMATION; PARTICULARLY WITH REGARD TO THE TREATMENT OF BONES.

They (the Bushmen) put the things' bones nicely aside, while they do not throw them (about).

They put down the bones opposite to the entrance to the hut (the place which the. hut's mouth faces; they call it "the hut face's opposite"(?)); and they go they pour down the bones at it. Therefore, they call it, "The heap of meat bones[1]; while they feel that this is the place to which they go, at which they pour down the bones; they pour down the bones by the side of a bush (a little thorn bush), at the place to which they go to put down the bones.

And another person [who lives opposite] gnaws, putting the bones upon an (ostrich) breastbone;[2] he does as follows, when he has finished gnawing the bones, he takes up the bones, he goes to pour down the bones at this place.[3]

1. This heap of bones (springbok, gemsbok, hare, porcupine, etc.) is called |uhaiten as well as |ka.
2. The breastbone of an ostrich, used as a dish.
3. One hut has its own heap of bones; the other man also has the other man's heap of bones; another man also has his own heap of bones, the bones of the springbok. which he kills.

And when they have boiled other bones, they again gnaw,[1] putting them upon (the ostrich breastbone dish). When they have finished gnawing the bones, they take up the ostrich breastbone upon which the bones are, they go to pour down the bones opposite to the entrance to the other one's hut. The other one (i.e.

the neighbour living opposite) also when he has boiled, takes the bones which he gnaws, he goes to pour them down, opposite to the entrance of the other one's hut, (upon) the other one's heap of bones,² he goes to pour down the bones upon it. Another man also does thus, when he has gnawed the bones, he also goes to pour down the bones opposite to the entrance of the other one's hut, (upon) the other one's heap of bones.

And, they³ also (do it), a different man does

1. biting off the flesh from the bones. The heap of bones belonging to the other man who killed the springbok.
2. Another man (it) is. I think that he has a wife and children. These children are those for whom he cuts off meat. He cuts meat; he cuts off for this child (a boy) this piece of meat; he cuts off for this (other) child (also a boy) this (other) piece of meat while the woman cuts off meat for the little girl.
3. The women do not eat (the meat of) the springbok's shoulder blades, because they show respect for the men's arrows, so that the men may quietly kill. For, when we miss our aim, the place is not nice; for we are wont to be ill when we miss our aim; when we shoot destruction to ourselves, when we are going to be ill. Therefore we become ill.

   The springbok are in possession of (invisible) magic arrows (?). Therefore, we are ill on account of the springbok. Therefore, we do not allow the little children to play upon the springbok skin. For the springbolk is wont to get into our flesh, and we become ill. And the springbok is inside of us and we become ill on account of it. Therefore, we do not play tricks with springbok's bones; for we put the springbok's bones nicely away, while we feel that the springbok is wont to get into our flesh. The springbok also possesses things which are magic sticks; if they stand in us, we, being pierced, fall dead.

as follows, he also boils, he also gnaws, putting the bones upon an ostrich breastbone; he also comes to pour down the bones opposite to the entrance of the other one's hut.

They also do thus when they cut up a springbok, they also take out the stomach, as they, cutting open (the springbok), take out the stomach; they go to shake out the contents of the stomach opposite to the entrance of the other one's hut; they go to shake out the contents of the stomach there (upon the other one's heap of bones). They [having washed it well] come to lade blood into the stomach, they dip up blood with their band,¹ they lade blood into the stomach with their hand, while they turn with their band (holding the right hand like a scoop); they holding, form a tortoise [shell] with their hand. With regard to the blood which has spilt,² that which lies upon the earth, they also take it up (with the earth on which it lies), together with the bushes[3] upon which there is blood; they go to put them down opposite to the entrance of the other man's hut (the hut of the man who, killed the springbok).

With regard to the |*kaoken* bones,[4] from which the children (breaking them) eat out the marrow, they also collect them together; they go to put them down opposite to the entrance of the other one's hut.

With regard to the shoulder blade bones, when they have gnawed them, they put them away in the

1. One hand.
2. It is blood which lies (*lit.* "sits") upon the ground.
3. They lay the springbok on the bushes.
4. Springbok's bones.

hut;[1] because they desire that the dogs may not crunch them; while they feel that the other man (who shot the springbok) would miss his aim.

They take to the other man (who shot the springbok) the upper bones of the fore legs, while they intend that the other man's child shall go (and) eat out the marrow from them; for the other man was the one who killed the springbok. Therefore they take to the other man the upper bones of the fore leg. The shoulder blade bones which they gnaw, they put away in the sticks of the hut, they are those into which they put them.

They cut off the back of the springbok's neck, they take it to the other man (who killed the springbok); while they boil the springbok's back, they gnaw its bones, together with the tail, which they wish the wife to put away, that the wife may, rubbing, make soft for him bags, that he may go to get things, when he bartering goes to another man; he goes to give them to another man, when the wife has rubbed, making soft for him, springbok skin bags. The wife rubs, making them soft for him; he folds them up, he lays them into (his own) bag, and he goes to the other man.

They (the man and his wife) go, to give them to the other man; and the other person (that is, the other man's wife) also gives her (the first man's wife) *tto*,[2] which is red; she also gives some ||*hara* with the *tto*, because the other one (the first man's wife) gave the other bags.

155

Then, the man also gives to the other man his own bags, he who is the man, his own bags. And the

1. In a paper published in the *Westminster Reveiw* (New Series, no cvii, July 1878, ii. "The Mythology and Religious Worship of the Ancient Japanese"), it is stated that the Japanese used the shoulder blade of a deer for the purpose of divination; and that Pallas found a similar practice among the Kirghiz, by whom the shoulder blade of a sheep was employed.

 [In Staffordshire, also, sixty years ago, the shoulder blade bone of a sheep was believed to possess the power of fortelling the future—ED.
2. For a little further inforination regarding *tto* and | |*hara* see IX.—237.

other man also gives him arrows; because he (the man who brought the bags) wishes that the other man may give him in exchange poisoned arrows, that the other man may give him in exchange poison (i.e. poisoned arrows). Therefore, the other man gives him in exchange poison.

TREATMENT OF BONES BY THE NARRATOR'S GRANDFATHER, TSATSI.

Thus my grandfather (Tsatsi) was one who put away (in the sticks of the hut) the upper bones of the fore leg, and the shoulder blades, and the springbok's ||*khurken*; because the first finger (of our right hand) is apt to get a wound when we are shooting, if the dogs eat the springboks' ||*khu*||*khuruken*, our first finger has a wound; we do do not know how to manage with it, when we pull the string as we are shooting.

Therefore, we sew our first finger into a cover(?) (it is skin which has been rubbed and made soft), which the wife cuts out, she sews it for us; we put our finger into it; and then we pull the (bow-) string, while we feel that our finger is inside. We are shooting, when we lie in wait for the springbok. Then it is that our finger gets a wound, when we shoot, lying in the screen of bushes, while the springbok come up to tis as we lie, because the springbok are not a little numerous, when we have gone by night (among tliem, making a shelter behind which to shoot). Therefore, this male springbok, he comes out from this place, he walks, coming up to us, we shall shoot (him). He runs away, he goes to lie down (to die), while we lie inside the screen of bushes which we have made.

HOW THE FATHER-IN-LAW OF THE NARRATOR TREATED BONES.

"Dream" was the one who threw bones upon a heap; therefore, I did so, while I felt that I had married into them (i.e. into the family).

I threw the bones upon a heap, (and gave the shoulder blade bones to the dogs, while I felt that my father-in-law, Dream," was the one who did thus. Therefore, Smoke's Man" (the son of "Dream") does the same.

TACTICS IN SPRINGBOK HUNTING.

This man [who stands at 5], he has ostrich feathers upon sticks.[1] Therefore, he sticks (into the little bushes) a large stick with ostrich feathers (upon it) here [at 6], because he wants it to look like a man who stands, so that the spriugbok may see it, when they go towards the (lesser) feather brushes. For, the springbok would (otherwise), turning back, pass behind him, when he was driving[2] the springbok for the other people, the springbok would, turning back, pass behind him, at the place where he

1. The !Xui!Xui are three in number; of these he sticks two (a longer and a shorter) into the ground at 6 and 7; the smallest of the three he holds in his hand, waving it over his head to make the springbok afraid of him. He had been calling the springbok; but is now silent; because the springbok have come into the curve of the feather brushes.
2. (He) drives the springbok, that they may run in among the other people. He does not a little run along, for, he passes the foremost springbok, while he desires that the springbok may not pass by on one side of the man who came to lie on this side.

had stood, calling them. He runs forward from it. Therefore, he sticks in a feather brush at it [at 6]. He goes, also to stick in a little feather brush, which is short [at 7]; while he intends, with the little feather brush which is very small to drive the springbok, as he wishes that the foremost one may run, passing through, may run passing by the man who lies between [at 9]; he is the one to whom he (the man who drives the springbok) intends the foremost to run.[1] Therefore, the springbok do thus, when this man shoots the springbok which follows the leading one, they divide nicely; because, the 'springbok which was following the other turns aside, it darts aside, while the springbok which had been following it turns aside [in an opposite direction], while they, springing aside, divide at the noise of the arrow on the other one's skin, that and (the noise of) the feathers, which went so quickly.

1. [At 8 is] the man who lies . . . ; the inan who lies to leeward. He lies "with a red head".

VIII. PERSONAL HISTORY.

||KABBO'S CAPTURE AND JOURNEY TO CAPE TOWN. FIRST ACCOUNT.

I came from that place, I came (here), when I came from my place, when I was eating a springbok. The Kafir took me; he bound my arms. We (that is, I) and my son, with my daughter's husband, we were three, when we were bound opposite to (?) the wagon, while the wagon stood still. We went away bound to the Magistrate; we went to talk with him; we remained with him.

We were in the jail. We put our legs into the stocks. The Korannas came to us, when our legs were in the stocks; we were stretched out(?) in the stocks. The Korannas came to put their legs into the stocks; they slept, while their legs were in the stocks. They were in the house of ordure(?). While we were eating the Magistrate's sheep, the Korannas came to eat it. We all ate it, we and the Korannas.

We went; we ate sheep on the way, while we were coming to Victoria; our wives ate their sheep on the way, as they came to Victoria.

We came to roll stones at Victoria, while we worked at the road. We lifted stones with our chests; we rolled great stones. We again worked with earth. We carried earth, while the earth was upon the handbarrow. We carried earth; we loaded the wagon with earth; we pushed it. Other people walked along. We were pushing the wagon's wheels; we were pushing; we poured down the earth; we pushed it back. We again loaded it, we and the Korannas. Other Korannas were carrying the handbarrow. Other people (i.e. Bushmen) were with the Korannas; they were also carrying earth;

while the earth was upon the handbarrow. They again came to load the handbarrow with earth.

We again had our arms bound to the wagon chain; we walked along, while we were fastened to the wagon chain, as we came to Beaufort, while the sun was hot. They (our arms) were set free in the road. We got tobacco from the Magistrate; we smoked, going along, with sheeps' bones. We came into Beaufort jail. The rain fell upon us, while we were in Beaufort jail.

Early (the next) morning, our arms were made fast, we were bound. We splashed into the water; we splashed, passing through the water in the river bed. We walked upon the road, as we followed the wagon, while the wagon went first. We walked, following the wagon, being bound, until we, being bound, came to the Breakwater. On the way, we ate sheep as we came to the Breakwater; we came (and) worked at it.

A white man took us to meet the train in the night. We early sat in the train; the train ran, bringing us to the Cape. We came into the Cape prison house when we were tired, we and the Korannas; we lay down to sleep at noon.

||KABBO'S CAPTURE AND JOURNEY TO CAPE TOWN. SECOND ACCOUNT.

My wife was there; I was there; my son was there; my son's wife was there, while she carried a little child (on her back); my daughter was there, while she also carried a little child; my daughter's husband was there; we were like this (in number). Therefore, the Kafirs[1] took (lit. "lifted") us, when we were like this, while we were not numerous; the Kafirs took us, while we were not numerous.

We went to sit in the wagon; the Kafirs took us away, as we sat in the wagon. Our wives also sat in the wagon. They got out of the wagon; they walked upon their feet. The wagon stood still; we got out of the wagon; we lay down, when we had first made a fire. We roasted lamb's flesh; my son)s wife roasted a springbok, which I had killed with my arrow. We smoked; we lay down. The day broke; we made a fire; we smoked early in the morning.

Then, we left them, we went away to the Magistrate; while we (who were in the wagon) ran along, we were upon the road, while our wives walked along upon their feet. We ran, leaving them, while we altogether ran, leaving them.

1. Kafir police are probably meant here.

Then we went to talk with the Magistrate; the Magistrate talked with us. The Kafirs took us away to the jail at night. We went to put our legs into the stocks; another white man laid another (piece of) wood upon our legs. We slept, while our legs were in the stocks. The day broke, while our legs were in the stocks. We early took out our legs from the stocks, we ate meat; we again put our legs into the stocks; we sat, while our legs were in the stocks. We lay down, we slept, while our legs were inside the stocks. We arose, we smoked, while our legs were inside the stocks. The people boiled sheep's flesh, while our legs were in the stocks.

The Magistrate came to take our legs out of the stocks, because he wished that we might sit comfortably, that we might eat; for, it was his sheep that we were eating. *Katteng* ("Piet Rooi") came (and) ate with us of the Magistrate's sheep, while we were eating it; also another man, *Khabbi-ddau*, also *!kwarra-ga-|k(e)ow*.

They again put their legs into the stocks; they slept, while their legs were in the stocks. Other Korannas also came, they came into another house, another "jail's house."

||KABBO'S JOURNEY IN THE RAILWAY TRAIN.[1]

I have said to thee that the train (fire wagon) is nice. I sat nicely in the train. We two sat in (it), we (I) and a black man.

A woman did seize my arm; she drew me inside, because I should have fallen, therefore she drew me in. I sat beside a black man; his face was black; his mouth (was) also black; for they are black.

White men are those whose faces are red, for they are handsome. The black man he is ugly, thus his mouth is black, for his face is black.

The black man then asked me: "Where dost thou come from?" I said to the black man: "I come from this place." The black man asked me: "What is its name?" I said to the blackman: "My place is the Bitterpits."

1. From Mowbray to Cape Town and back.

||KABBO'S INTENDED RETURN HOME.

Thou knowest that I sit waiting for the moon to turn back for me, that I may return to my place.

That I may listen to all the people's stories, when I visit them; that I may listen to their stories, that which they tell; they listen to the Flat Bushmen's stories from the other side of the place. They are those which they thus tell,[1] they are listening to them; while the other !Xoe-ssho-!kui (the sun) becomes a little warm, that I may sit in the sun; that I may sitting, listen to the stories which yonder come (?), which are stories which come from a distance.[2] Then; I shall get hold of a story from them, because they (the stories) float out from a distance; while the sun feels a little warm; while I feel that I must altogether visit; that I may be talking with them, my fellow men.

For, I do work here, at women's household work. My fellow men are those who are listening to stories from afar, which float along; they are listening to stories from other places. For, I am here; I do not obtain stories; because I do not visit, so that I might hear stories which float along; while I feel that the people of another place are here; they do not possess my stories. They do not talk my language; for, they visit their like; while they feel that work's people (they) are, those who work, keeping houses in order. They work (at) food; that the food may grow for them; that they should get food which is good, that which is new food.

The Flat Bushmen go to each other's huts; that they may smoking sit in front of them. Therefore, they obtain stories at them; because

---

1. With the stories of their own part of the country too.
2. ||kabbo explains that a story is "like the wind, it comes from a far-off quarter, and we feel it."

they are used to visit; for smoking's people they are. As regards myself (?) I am waiting that the moon may turn back for me; that I may set my feet forward in the path.[1] For, I verily(?) think that I must only await the moon; that I may tell my Master (*lit.* chief), that I feel this is the time when I should sit among my fellow men, who walking meet their like. They are hstening to them; for, I do think of visits; (that) I ought to visit; (that) I ought to talk with my fellow men; for, I work here, together with women; and I do not talk with them; for, they merely send me to work.

I must first sit a little, cooling my arms; that the fatigue may go out of them; because I sit. I do merely listen, watching for a story, which I want to hear; while I sit waiting for it; that it may float into my ear.[2] These are those to which I am listening with all my ears; while I feel that I sit silent. I must wait (listening) behiiad me,[3] while I listen along the road; while I feel that my name floats along the road; they (my three names)[4] float along to my place; I will go to sit at it; that I may listening turn backwards (with my ears) to my feet's heels, on which I went; while I feel that a story is the wind. It (the story)

1. When a man intends to turn back, he steps turning (?) round, he steps going backwards.
2. The people's stories.
3. ||*kabbo* explains that, when one has travelled along a road, and goes and sits down, one waits for a story to travel to one, following one along the same road.
4. "Jantje," |*uhi-ddoro*, and ||*kabbo*.

is wont to float along to another place. Then, our names do pass through those people; while they do not perceive our bodies go along. For, our names are those which, floating, reach a different place. The mountains lie between (the two different roads). A man's name passes behind the mountains' back; those (names) with which he returning goes along. While he (the man) feels that the road is that which lies thus; and the man is upon it. The road is around his place, because the road curves. The people who dwell at another place, their ear does listening go to meet the returning man's names; those with which he returns.[1] He will examine the place. For, the trees of the place seem to be handsome; because they have grown tall; while the man of the place (||*kabbo*) has not seen them, that he might walk among them. For, he came to live at a different place;

his place it is not. For, it was so with him that people were those who brought him to the people's place, that he should first come to work for a little while at it. He is the one who thinks of (his) place, that he must be the one to return.

He only awaits the return of the moon; that the moon may go round, that he may return (home), that he may examine the water pits; those at which he drank. He will work, putting the old hut in order, while he feels that he has gathered his children together, that they may work, putting the water in order for him; for, he did go away, leaving the place, while strangers were those who walked at the place. Their place it is not; for ||*kabbo*'s father's father's place it was.

1. ||*kabbo* explains that the people know all the man's names.

And then ||*kabbo*'s father did possess it; when ||*kabbo*'s father's father died, ||*kabbo*'s father was the one who possessed it. And when ||*kabbo*'s father died, ||*kabbo*'s elder brother was the one who possessed the place; ||*kabbo*'s elder brother died, (then) ||*kabbo*'s possessed the place.[1] And then ||*kabbo* married when grown up, bringing ||*kabba-ang* to the place, because he felt that he was alone; therefore, he grew old with his wife at the place, while he felt that his children were married. His children's[2] children talked, they, by themselves, fed themselves; while they felt that they talked with understanding.

Therefore, they (||*kabbo*'s children) placed huts for themselves; while they felt that they made huts for themselves; they made their huts nicely; while my hut stood alone, in the middle; while they (my children) dwelt on either side. Because my elder brother's child (Betje) married first, they (my own children) married afterwards; therefore, their cousin's child grew up first; while she (the cousin) felt that she married, leaving me; she who, from afar, travelling came to me; because

1. |*hang#kass'o* (son-in-law of ||*kabbo*) gave in July, 1878, the following description of ||*kabbo*'s place, ||*gubo*, or Blauwputs."

People (that is Bastaards) call it "Blauwputs" while they feel that its rocks are black; for, they are slate.

||*kabbo*'s place is ||*gubo*; and he altogether went round, he, possessing, went along at the place; thus, he possessed *!khui-tteng* and ||*Xau-ka-!khoa*. He possessed

||*Xuobbeten* (a certain water pool); and, he, altogether possessing, went along, he possessed |*unn.*

Therefore, he dug out (at) ||*ka-ttu* [the name of a place near ||!*gubo*]. He dug, making a (deep) pitfall (for game), there. Therefore, an ostrich was slaughtered at that pitfall, because my father-in-law's pitfalls were surpassingly good ones.

2. The word @*puondde* here means both ||*kabbo*'s son and daughter.

I was the one who feeding, brought her up. Her father was not the one who liad fed her. For, her father died, leaving her. I was the, one who went (and) fetched her, when her mother had just died; I brought her to my home. As I felt that I had not seen her father die,[1] I also did not see her mother die; for, her mother too, died,[2] leaving her; I only heard the story.

And then I went to fetch her (Betje), while I felt that I was still a young man, and I was fleet in running to shoot. And I thought that she would get plenty of food, which 1 should give her. She (would) eat it. She (would) eat with my (own) child, which was still (an only) one. And then they would both grow, going out from me (to play near the hut); because they both ate my game ("shot things"). For, I was fresh for running; I felt that I could, running, catch things.

Then I used to run (and) catch a hare, I brought

1. The father was killed by some one who was angry with him, while he himself was not angry; he had been visiting at anothr house, and had slept five nights away from home. A man who was at that place where his wife lived, gave the child food, but it still cried after its own father. The man was angry witht the father, because he had stayed away from his wife, ||*kabo* says, and because the child still cried for him. And, when the father had returned, and was sleeping by the side his wife, in his own hut, the man came behind the hut in the very early morning, and stabbed him as he slept, with a Kafir assegai, which had be bought at Wittberg. As he lay dead in the hut, the rest (including his wife) left him, by the advice of the murderer.
2. The mother died afterwards of some internal sickenss; she was not buried, because, at the time of her death, she only had a younger sister with her, who was suffering from the same illness. The latter went away with difficulty, taking the dead mother's child to a relative's hut, not near at hand. From the relative's but, the fire of |*kabo*'s dwelling could be seen at night. She proceeded thither with the child, and was met by him midway. Before he got the child, he had seen the dead mother's bones lying at her hut, her body having just been eaten by jackals. ||*kabo* had gone off from his home in baste, hearing that the wife's sister was ill, and fearing that she might die on the way, and the child, yet living and playing about, might be devoured by jackals. He left his own home early one morning, and in the evening reached the spot where the mother's bones lay. He made a hut at a little distance, and slept there one night, and the next morning went to fetch the child at the relation's hut; but the sister met him with it on the road. He slept at the newly-made hut, to which he returned with the child, for one more night, and then went back to his own home.

it to my home, while it was in my bag, while the sun was hot. I felt that I had not seen a springbok. For, I saw a hare. I used to shoot, sending up a bustard. I put it in(to the bag) (and) brought it home. My wife would come to pluck it, at home. She boiled it in the pot; that we might drink soup. On the morrow I would hunt the hare, I would be peeping about in the shade of the bushes. I would shoot it up,[1] that the children might eat. For, the springbok were gone away. Therefore, I was shooting hares, that I might chasing, cause them to die with the sun, when they had run about in the noonday's sun. They were "burnt dead" by the sun; while I remembered that the hare does not drink; for it eats dry bushes, while it does not drink, putting in water upon the dry bushes which it crunches. Therefore, it remains thirsty there, while it does not drink. It dwells, sitting in the summer (heat), because it does not understand water pans, so that it might go to the water, so that it might go to drink. For it waits, sitting in the sun.

Therefore, I chase it, in the sun, that the sun may, burning, kill it for me, that I may eat it, dead from the sun; while I feel that I was the one who chased it, while it went along in fear of me. It, in fear, lay down to die from the sun; because it had become dry (while running about) in the sun; because it saw me when I followed it. It did not stop to walk, that it might look backwards. For it had run about, when it was tired.

1. *i.e.*, make it spring up from its form and run away, falling down dead later.

It seemed as if it were about (?) to die; because it had been obliged to run about. Therefore, it went to lie down to die; because fatigue had killed it; while it had run about in the heat; for, (it) was the summer sun, which was hot. The ground was hot which was burning its feet.

Therefore, I used to go to pick it up, as it lay dead. I laid it in the arrows' bag. I must, going along, look for another hare. It would spring up (running) into the sun; it would, being afraid, run through the sun, while I ran following it. I must, going along, wait, so that the sun might, burning, kill it. I would go to pick it up, when it lay dead. I would sitting, break its (four) legs, and then I should put it in. I thought that another hare would probably dwell opposite to it. I must first go to seek round in the neighbourliood of the form. For it seemed to be married. I must, seeking around, look for the female hare, that I might also chase it, when I had unloosened (and) laid down the bag. I must chase it, with my body. I must run very fast, feeling that I should become thirsty.

I shall go to drink at home.[1] For the children will have probably fetched[2] water. For, my wife (was) used to send them to the water, thinking that I had walked about in the sun when the sun was hot; because I thought that |*kui*[3] would kill the

1. Water which is in an ostrich eggshell.
2. In the ostrich eggshells, and probably also in a springbok's stomach.
3. Also called "gambro"; a vegetable food eaten by Bushmen; which is injurious if used as the chief nourishaient in winter, causing severe pain in the head and singing in the ears.

children for me. The rain must first fall, and then, I should be looking around, while I looked around, seeking for (a pair of) ostriches which are wont to seek the water along the "Har Rivier", that they may, going along, drink the water. I must, going round in front, descend into the "Har Rivier".

I must (in a stooping position) steal up to them in the inside of the river bed. I must lie (on the front of my body) in the river bed; that I might shoot, lying in the river bed. For, the western ostriches do, seeking water, come back; that they may, going along, drink the new water.

Therefore, I must sit waiting for the Sundays on which I reinain here, on which I continue to teach thee. I do not again await another moon, for this moon is the one about which I told thee. Therefore, I desired that it should do thus, that it should return for me. For I have sat waiting for the boots, that I must put on to walk in; which are strong for the road. For, the sun will go along, burning strongly. And then, the earth becomes hot, while I still am going along halfway. I must go together with the warm sun, while the ground is hot. For, a little road it is not. For, it is a great road; it is long. I should reach my place, when the trees are dry. For, I shall walk, letting the flowers become dry while I still follow the path.

Then, autumn will quickly be (upon) us there; when I am sitting at my (own) place. For, I shall not go to other places; for, I must remain at my (own) place, the name of which I have told my Master; he knows it; be knows, (having) put it

1. When he is sitting at his own place.

down. And thus my name is plain (beside) it. It is there that I sit waiting for the gun; and then, he will send the gun to me there; while he sends the gun in a cart; that which running, takes me the gun. While he thinks, that I have not forgotten; that my body may be quiet, as it was when I was with him; while I feel that I shoot, feeding myself. For, starvation was that on account of which I was bound, starvation's food,-when I starving turned back from following the sheep. Therefore, I lived with him, that I might get a gun from him; that I might possess it. That I might myself shoot, feeding myself, while I do not eat my companions' food. For, I eat my (own) game.

For, a gun is that which takes care of an old man; it is that with which we kill the springbok which go through the cold (wind); we go to eat, in the cold (wind). We do, satisfied with food, lie down (in our huts) in the cold (wind). It (the gun) is strong against the wind. It satisfies a man with food in the very middle of the cold.

HOW |HANG#KASS'O'S PET LEVERET WAS KILLED.

|*Xabbi-ang*[1] killed (my) leveret for me, and I came crying to her, because I wanted them[2] therefore to seek for (other) leverets; for they were those who had killed (my) leveret for me. And she soothed

1. The narrator's mother.
2. *i.e.* his mother and his maternal grandmother #*kammi*.

me, about it. Therefore, she told me that the lizard had formerly said:

"For,
I therefore intend to go,
Passing through,
guru-|na's pass.—
"For,
I therefore intend to go,
Passing through,
|*Xe-!khwai*'s pass."

Tsatsi[1] was the one who caught hold of (and) took up a leveret on the hunting-ground; and, he brought it (home) alive, he came (and) gave it to me. And I played with it; I set it down, it ran; I also ran after it. And I went to catch it, and, I came to set it down. It again ran; and I again ran to catch it; and I went catching hold of it, I came to set it down. Again, it ran; and, I again ran after it. And I again caught hold of it; and again, I caught hold of it; and I came to set it down.

|*Xabbi-aṅ* wished that I (should) leave off playing with the leveret, that I (should) kill it, that I (should) lay it to roast. I was not willing to kill the leveret. She wished me to leave off playing with the leveret, that I (should) kill it, that I might lay it to roast. I was not willing to kill the leveret, because I felt that nothing acted as prettily as it did, when it was gently running, gently running along. It did in this manner (showing the motion of its ears), while it was gently running along, nothing acted as prettily as it did; and it went to sit down.

1. The narrator's maternal grandfather.

Then they told me to fetch water; for I was one who quickly came away from the water, while I did not go to play at the water. Therefore, I went to fetch water, when I had tied up the leveret. And I went to fetch water; then, they killed (my) leveret for me, while I was at the water. They killed (my) leveret for me; and then I came (and) cried, about it; because I had thought that they would let (my) leveret alone. For, they must have been deceiving me; they told me to fetch water, while they must have intended that they would kill (my) leveret for me, which I had meant to let alone, so that it might live (on) in peace. They had killed it for me. Therefore, I came (and) cried, on account of it. They said, that we should not again get another leveret; when I wanted them to seek some leverets for me, they said, we should not again get another leveret.

Therefore, they soothing calmed(?) me with the (story of the) lizard; while they wished that I might quietly listen to them; when I had shut my mouth, I might quietly listen to them.[1]

1. She (my mother) said (to me), that I should not play with meat; for we do not play with meat; for we lay meat to roast. For the leveret is not a little fat; therefore, we kill it, we lay it to roast, while we do not play with it.

THE THUNDERSTORM.

When the rain fell upon us at night, I did thus, while the rain fell, I lay, playing the "goura",[1] like

1. A description of this musical instrument will be found on p. 100 of "The Native Races of South Africa", by the late Mr. G. W. Stow (London, 1905), and a picture of it in the preceding plate (fig. 8).

||*kunn*.[1] And mamma said to me, did I not see how the rain was lightening; that I did like ||*kunn*; did I not know that ||*kunn* was a person who used, if people scolded him, he used, (when) he was angry with the people, to say to the people, about it, that the people seemed to think that the rain would fall; but (on the contrary) the rain would stand still, while the rain did not fall. The rain-used really to stop; when ||*kunn* had said that the rain would not fall.

When mamma rebuked me, I did not listen to her, for, I lay, playing the "goura", like ||*kunn*. And mamma became silent; when she saw that I did not seem as if I heard her. And mamma lay down; I lay, playing the "goura".

And the rain did thus, as I lay, playing the "goura", the rain first seemed to shine into our eyes. And the rain did thus, (when) we were thinking that it was going to lighten and it seemed as if the rain were closing our eyes, when it was the light that entered. our eyes; we stood shutting our eyes, while we felt as if darkness kept our eyes closed. And when we had not (yet) opened our eyes, the rain gave us things on account of which our eyes seemed as if they were green; and the rain lightened, while our eyes felt green.

And the rain, lightening, went over us; and the rain did as follows to a stone which stood outside, in front of our hut, the rain, lightening, shivered it.

And mamma exclaimed: "*Ng ng ng ng ng!*" And father questioned mamma, as to what was the matter

1. ||*kunn* or "Coos Groot-Oog "was a rain sorcerer, wbo lived at !*khai* |*ku* (also called "Evvicass Pits", on account of a tree which stands by the Pits).

with her; had the rush of the storm[1] reached her that she exclaimed as if in pain? And mamma told father about it, that) the thing seemed as if the rain were tearing off her skin; therefore, she had exclaimed with pain. And mamma said that we had wished to fall dead; it was our fault that we had not been willing to obey her when she rebuked us about a very little thing. We had wanted to see (what would happen) when we did not appear to hear when she rebuked us.

I had acted thus, when mamma told me to leave off playing the "goura",-like ||*kunn*,—I would not listen; I was the one who saw that the rain had intended to kill us, on account of my doings.

1. The narrator compares this to the wind from a cannon ball.

IX. CUSTOMS AND SUPERSTITIONS.

CUTTING OFF THE TOP OF THE LITTLE FINGER, AND PIERCING EARS AND NOSE.

A little boy has this hand out.[1] A female child has this hand cut,[2] because she is a little girl, therefore, she has the hand of her female arm cut; because this is her female hand. The little boy feels that he is a little boy, therefore, he has this hand cut, his male arm, for, they shoot with this hand. Another boy does not have his hand cut; another girl does not have her hand cut.

Thus, the boy has this arm cut, with which they intend him to shoot; therefore, he turns this (the right) hand, when be grasps the arrow, he turns this (the left) hand, when he grasps the bow.

Another man has this (the right) ear pierced; he also has that (the left) ear pierced. Another woman has this (the left) ear pierced, because she feels that her female arm is here (ie. on this side); she also has this (the right) ear pierced, because she feels that her male arm is here; she also has her nose pierced.

Another woman does not have her nose pierced, because the other woman is ugly; the other woman who has had her nose pierced, is handsome.

1. Showing the top joint of the little finger of the right hand.
2. Showing the top joint of the little finger of the left hand.

CUTTING OFF THE TOP OF THE LITTLE FINGER.

SECOND ACCOUNT.

Her father, |*Ukwaiyau*, was the one who cut off the upper joint of his daughter *Kaueten-ang*'s little finger.[1]

My husband was the one who cut off (the upper joint of) !*kabbe-tu*'s ("Willem Streep's") finger.

1. |*Xaken-ang* further explained that the joint is cut off with reed. It is thought to make children live to grow up. It is done before they suck at all.

BUSHMAN PRESENTIMENTS[2]

The Bushmen's letters[3] are in their bodies. They (the letters) speak, they, move, they make their (the Bushmen's) bodies move. They (the Bushmen) order the others to be silent a man is altogether still, when he feels that his body is tapping (inside). A dream speaks falsely, it is (a thing) which deceives. The presentiment is that which speaks the truth; it is that by means of which the Bushman gets (or perceives) meat, when it has tapped.

3. The above piece of Bushman native literature is described by Dr. Bleek as follows: "99. Bushman Presentiments.—They feel in their bodies that certain events are going to happen. There is a kind of beating of the flesh, which tells them things. Those who are stupid, do not understand these teachings; they disobey them, and get into trouble,—such as being killed by a lion, etc.—The beatings tell those who understand them, which way they are not to go, and which arrow they had better not use, and also warn them, when many people are coming to the house on a wagon. They inform people where they can find the person of whom they are in search, *i.e.*, which way they must go to seek him successfully." ("A Brief Account of Bushman Folk-lore and other Texts." By W.H.I. Bleek, Ph.D. Cape Town, 1875. pp. 17 and 18.)

2. The word !gwe was used by the Bushmen to denote both letters and books. ||kabbo explained that the beatings in their bodies, here described, are the Bushmen's "letters", and resemble the letters which take a message or an account of what happens in another place.

The Bushmen perceive people coming by means of it. The Bushmen feel a tapping (when) other people are[1] coming.

With regard to an old wound, a Bushman feels a tapping at the wound's place, while the tapping feels that the man (who has the old wound) walks, moving his body. The one man feels the other man who comes; he says to the children: "Look ye around, for grandfather, for grandfather seems to be coming; this is why I feel the place of his body's old wound." The children look around; the children perceive the man coming. They say to their father: "A man is coming yonder." Their father says to them: "Grandfather (his own father) comes yonder; he would come to me; he was the one whose coming I felt at the place of his old wound. I wanted you to see that he is really coming. For ye contradict my presentiment, which speaks truly."

He feels a tapping (at) his ribs; he says to the children: "The springbok seem to be coming, for I feel the black hair (on the sides of the springbok). Climb ye the Brinkkop standing yonder, that ye may look around at all the places. For I feel the springbok sensation." The other man agrees with him: "I think (that) the children (should) do so;

1. The Bushman, when an ostrich is coming and is scratching the back of its neck with its foot, feels the tapping in the lower part of the back of his own neck; at the same place where the ostrich is scratching.

    The springbok, when coming, scratches itself with its horns, and with its foot; then the Bushman feels the tapping.
2. When a woman who had gone away is returning to the house, the man who is sitting there, feels on his shoulders the thong with which the woman's child is slung over her shoulders; he feels the sensation there.

for the springbok come in the sun; for the Brinkkop standing yonder is high; they shall look down upon the ground. And then they can see the whole ground. They can therefore (?) look inside the trees; for the springbok are wont to go hidden inside the trees. For the trees are numerous. The little river beds are also there. They are those to which the springbok are wont to come (in order) to eat in them. For, the little river beds have become green.[1] For I am wont to feel thus, I feel a sensation in the calves of my legs when the springbok's blood is going to run down them. For I always feel blood, when I am about to kill springbok. For I sit feeling a sensation behind my back, which the blood is wont to run down, when I am carrying a springbok. The springbok hair lies behind my back." The other agrees with him (saying): Yes, my brother.

Therefore, we are wont to wait (quietly); when the sensation is like this, when we are feeling the things come, while the things come near the house. We have a sensation in our feet, as we feel the rustling of the feet of the springbok with which the springbok come, making the bushes rustle. We feel in this manner, we have a sensation in our heads, when we are about to chop the springbok's horns. We have a sensation in our face, on account of the blackness of the stripe on the face of the springbok;[2] we feel a sensation in our eyes, on account of the black marks on the eyes of the springbok. The ostrich is one, for whom we feel the sensation of

1. *i.e.*, the grass and the little bushes of the river bed.
2. A black stripe that comes down in the centre of the forehead, and terminates at the end of the nose.

a louse;[1] as it walks, scratching the louse; when it is spring,[2] when the sun feels thus, it is warm.

Then it is that the things go from us. They go along, passing opposite to the hut. Therefore, we early cross the things' spoor, when we early go to hunt. For, the things which are numerous are us, to come first, when we are lying in the shade of the hut; because they think that we are probably lying asleep in the noonday's sleep. For we really lie down to sleep the noonday's sleep. But we do not lie sleeping at noon, when we feel this sensation. For we are used to feel like this when the things are walking; when we have felt the things coming, as they walk, moving their legs. We feel a sensation in the hollows under our knees, upon which blood drops, as we go along, carrying (the game). Therefore, we feel this sensation there.

Therefore, the little boys do not lie in the shade inside the hut; they lie in the shade above yonder, so that they may beckon to us, when they have perceived the things, when the things walk at that place. They will beckon, making us see; for we are wont, sitting at a distance, to watch them, as they sit above yonder. Therefore, we say to each other, that the children appear to have seen things. For, they beckon. They point to that place, while they point to the place towards (?) which the things are walking, where the Brinkkop, mountains lie thus spread out (?). So we may quickly chase

1. An insect which bites the ostrich, a black insect; an "ostrich louse" as the Bushmen describe it.
2. | |*kabbo* explains that | |*gu* means "de bloem tijd."

the things at the hill which lies across, to which the things are walking. The things walk, putting themselves in front of it;[1] we will quickly pass behind it, while it still lies away (from the springbok). We will stand nicely (ready) for the things, that we may not steal up abreast[2] of the things, (but) that we may steal up in front of the things, at the place[3] to which the leader goes.

1. That is, putting their faces towards the mountain.
2. That is, not at the side of the game as it goes along, but right in front of its path.
3. The Bushmen are at the back of the hill, waiting for the springbok to cross it, coming to the place where they (the Bushmen) are.

DOINGS AND PRAYERS WHEN CANOPUS AND SIRIUS COME OUT.

The Bushmen perceive Canopus, they say to a child: "Give me yonder piece of wood, that I may put (the end of) it (in the fire), that I may point (it) burning (towards) grandmother, for, grandmother carries Bushman rice; grandmother shall make a little warmth for us; for she coldly comes out; the sun[1] shall warm grandmother's eye for us."

Sirius comes out; the people call out to one another: Sirius comes yonder; they say to one another Ye must burn (a stick) for us (towards) Sirius." They say to one another: "Who was it who saw Sirius?" One man says to the other: "Our brother saw Sirius." The other man says to him:

1. The sun is a little warm, when this star appears in winter.

I saw Sirius."[1] The other man says to him: "I wish thee to burn (a stick) for us (towards) Sirius; that the sun may shining come out f or us; that Sirius may not coldly come out." The other man (the one who saw Sirius) says to his son: "Bring me the (small) piece of wood yonder, that I may put (the end of) it (in the fire), that I may burn (it) towards grandmother; that grandmother may ascend the sky, like the other one, Canopus."

The child brings him the piece of wood, he (the father) holds (the end of) it in (the fire). He points (it) burning towards Sirius; he says that Sirius shall twinkle like Canopus. He sings; he sings (about) Canopus, he sings (about) Sirius; he points to them with fire,[2] that they may twinkle like each other. He throws fire at them. He covers himself up entirely (including his head) in (his) kaross and lies down.

He arises, he sits down; while he does not again lie down; because he feels that he has worked, putting Sirius into the sun's warmth; so that Sirius may warmly come out.

The women go out early to seek for Bushman rice; they walk, sunning their shoulder blades.[3]

1. ||*Ukoa-ggu*, "Canopus," and *!kuttau*, "Sirius," are both female stars, ||*kabbo* says.
2. With the stick that he had held in the fire, moving it up and down quickly.
3. They take one arm out of their kaross, thereby exposing one shoulder blade to the sun.

THE MAKING OF CLAY POTS.

The women dig, removing the earth which lies above, lif ting it away; and they only dig out the earth[1] which is inside there. And they scoop it out; they put it into the bag. And they sling it (the earth) over their [left] shoulder, they take it home.

And, as they return, they go along plucking grass, they only pluck the male grass; they bind it together. And they take it to the hut.

And they pound the pot (clay),[2] pound (it), making it soft.[3] And they pound the grass, they also pound, making the grass soft. And they put the grass into the earth; and they make the earth wet. And they make the earth wet, and they make the earth very nice indeed, and they mould[4]

1. The earth resembles stones which contain things which seem to glitter. Hence, the earth of which the people make a pot contains things, which are like them (i.e., like the said glittering particles). The earth is red,
    The earth to which the people go, to dig it out, is red. They call it "a pot's hole", because they dig, making a stick's hole, there. Therefore, they call it "a pot's hole".
2. The earth of which they make the pot.
    It is earth; it is dry; the people pound it (when) it is dry. And they sift it, sift out the earth which is soft. And they pour down the earth which is hard [to be pounded again at another time]. With regard to the soft earth, they pour it out upon a skin [a whole skin, which has no holes in it, a springbok skin].
3. Pound, making it like sand. (They) put it upon a skin.
4. They work it; they work, making a pot of it.

the earth. And, when they have made the lower part of the pot, they, holding, break off the clay, they rub the clay between their hands. They put the clay down (in a circle). And they smooth[1] the clay very nicely indeed; they moulding, raise (the sides of) the pot. And they smooth it, smooth it, smooth it, make it very nice indeed, they set it down to dry (in the sun).[2] And they make a little pot which is small, beautiful beyond comparison. They anoint the pot with fat, while they wish the pot not to split. Therefore, they anoint the pot with fat, while the pot is still damp, when the pot has just newly dried, the pot's inner part (the inner layers, not the inside) being still damp; because they wish the pot to dry when it has fat upon it (inside and out). And they set the pot (in tile sun) to dry; they make a little pot; they make it very nicely indeed. They set the little pot to dry (in the sun) by the side of the large pot; and they take the other part of the clay; they make it also wet. They mould it; they mould it very nicely indeed; they set it down. They also make another little pot, a little pot which is larger (lit. "grown"). And they set it to dry (in the sun). When the pot dries, they also prepare gum;[3] they pound it (between stones); they pound it, they pound, making it fine. They take it up in their hand (and) put it into the pot; and they

1. This is done with a piece of bone called !kau or !au (See IX.-185, and also illustration.)
2. (They) wish that it may become dry.
3. The berries (lit. "the eyes") of the "Doorn Boom" are black (i.e. "black gum"). The people call them the dung of the "Doorn Boom", because they come out of the stem of the !khou tree.
4. A white gum, called !gui, seems also to be found on this tree.

pour in water [into the new pot]. It [the gum] boils while they feel that gum is that which adheres,[1] it resembles |kwaie.

And if springbok are at hand, a man kills a springbok, they pour the springbok's blood into (its) stomach, and the man brings back the blood he takes the blood home.

And the wife goes to pour the blood into the new pot. And she boils the blood; and, when the blood is cooked, she takes the pot off the fire, she takes the blood out of the pot (with a springbok horn spoon), and she sets the pot down; because she wishes the blood [ie., the blood remaining in the pot] to dry.

And she[2] again takes the pot, and she pours water into (it), she boils meat.

And, also, they do not strike with a stone,[3] when a new pot is on the fire, because they wish it not to split.

1. They smear the pot outside [with gum taken out with the spoon, made from springbok horn, with which they stir the gum which is boiling inside], while they wish this gum to adhere to the outsicle of the pot.

2. A man works at springbok's arrows, making them straight. A woman moulds pots.
3. |hang#kass'o further stated that his wife, Ssuobba-||keng, had been taught to make pots by |Xu-ang (an elder sister of her mother, !kuabba-ang), and also by |Xu-ang (another elder female relative on the maternal side).
3. To break bones (with a stone). The Bushmen do this because they do not possess an axe. They place a bone upon a stone which stands upon the ground, while they hold a stone which has a sharp edge, they strike with it; strike, dividing the bone because they intend to boil it, that they may gnaw it.

THE BUSHMAN SOUP SPOON.[1,2]

The hair of the Proteles is here, that part of the hair which is on the top of its back.[3] The roots of the hair are here, those which stick into the skin.

I do not know whether it is springbok's paxwax[4] [which binds the hair on the stick]. This is the (wood of the) "Driedoorn" (the "Driedoorn") is a bush.

We scratch the fire together with it (*i.e.*, with the handle of the brush). Therefore, the fire burns, blackening this part of it. It becomes black.

1. Among some Bushman implements given to Dr. Bleek. by a friend, was the brush of which a picture appears in the illustrations. ||*kabbo* recognized this at once as a Bushman "soup spoon" and showed us, with immense pleasure, in what manner the bushmen eat soup with it, and how well it can be used to take up the fat on the top of the soup, if rolled round in it.
2. The men are those who bind (i.e., make) them.
3. Really along its back, the narrator explains.
4. It is in the flesh; it lies upon the bone. It is yellow.

THE SHAPED RIB BONE.[1]

A bone (it) is; a rib (it.) is; a Bushman is the one who makes it.[2] He works it; he shapes it with a knife.

"Kambro" is that which we eat (with) it.

1. see illustration.
2. He works two ribs, with a knife.

THE BUSHMAN DRUM AND DANCING RATTLES.[1]

They tie, putting the bag over the pot's (drum's) mouth.[2] Then they tie on the sinew. And they pull the drum's siirface tight; for they wish that the drum may sound, when they beat the drum.

The men will tie springbok ears upon their feet;[3] they will dance, while the springbok ears sound, as springbok ears are wont to do, like what we call dancing rattles. Springbok ears (they) are; we call them dancing rattles. They sound well, when we have tied (them) on to our feet. They sound well, when we have tied (them) on to our feet. They sound well, they rattle as we dance, when we have tied (them) on to our feet. The drum which the women beat sounds well. Therefore, the men dance well on account of it, while they feel that the drum, which the women beat, sounds well. The dancing rattles which the men tie upon their feet sound well, because a woman who works nicely is the one who has worked them. Therefore, they sound nicely, beeause they are good. Therefore, they sound nicely, because they are good.

1. For a drawing of the dancing rattles see illustration.
2. A springbok's bag. They wet the skin of the springbok's thigh; then, when it is wet, they tie it over the pot's mouth and they try the drum.
3. Their insteps.

HOW THE DANCING RATTLES ARE PREPARED.

A woman takes off the skin[1] of the springbok's ear; and then, she sews the inner skin of the springbok's ear, when she has laid aside the (hairy) skin of the springbok's ear; for it is the inner skin of its ear which she sews. And she sews it, and she scoops up with her hand, putting soft earth into it. And they dig, lading in earth, because they wish that the springbok ears may dry; that they may put in ||*kerri*[2] berries when they have taken out the earth. And then they tie on a small piece of sinew at the tip of the springbok ear, which was open, while they tie shutting in the ||*kerri* berries, so that the ||*kerri* berries may not come out of the springbok ear. And they pierce through the springbok ears; and they put in little threads, which the men are to tie, fastening the springbok ears on their feet.[3]

1. The hairy skin.
2. The top of this plant is described as being like that of a pumpkin. Its seeds are black, and small. They are found underneath the flower, which is red. The root is roasted and eaten by the Bushmen. The seeds are also eaten, unroasted; being, when dry, pounded fine by the women with stones, and mixed with "Kambro" in order to moisten them for eating.
3. The narrator explains that the springbok ears, when thus prepared and filled, are tied, in fours or fives, on to the top of each foot (on the instep), letting the men's toes appear below them.

THE USE OF THE !GOING!GOING, FOLLOWED BY AN ACCOUNT OF A BUSHMAN DANCE.

The people beat the !going!going, (in order) that the bees may become abundant[1] for the people, (in order)

1. To become abundant.

that the bees may go into the other people's places, that the people may eat honey. Therefore, the people beat the !going!going, when they desire that the people's bees may go into the other people's places, so that the people may cut honey, that they may put honey away into bags.

And the people carry honey. And the people, carrying, bring the honey home. And the people take honey to the women at home. For, the women are dying of hunger, at home. Therefore, the men take honey to the women at home; that the women may go to eat, for they feel that the women have been hungry at home; while they wish that the women may make[1] a drum for them, so that they may dance, when the women are satisfied with food. For they do not frolic when they are hungry.

And they dance, when the women have made a drum for them. Therefore, the women make a drum for them; they dance. The men are those who dance, while the women sit down, because they clap their hands for the men when the men are those who dance; while one woman is the one who beats the drum; while many women are those who clap their hands for the men; because they feel that many men are dancing.

Then, the sun rises, while they are dancing there, while they feel that they are satisfied with food. Then, the sun rises, while they are dancing there, while they feel that the women are satisfied with food. Therefore, the sun shines upon the backs of

1. That the women may play for them, when the women are satisfied with food; that the women may also arrange the (game of) !goo for them, that they may roar.

their heads;[1] while the women get the dust of the drum. Then the men are covered (?) with dust, while the dust of the drum lies upon the women's faces, because the women are accustomed to sit down there; therefore, the dust of the drum lies upon the women's faces. Because they (the men) do not dance a little, for they dance very much. Therefore, their foot's dust covers the women's faces; because they have danced strongly. Therefore, they get their foot's dust, which rises up from their feet, it rises up among them, as they stand dancing. They dance, standing around, while the women are those who sit down, while the men are those who dance, standing around.

Therefore they sleep, letting the sun set;[2] because they are tired when they have been dancing there; while the women leave off drumming. Therefore they sleep, letting the sun set; because they are tired when they have been dancing there. Therefore, they sleep, letting the sun set; because they are tired when they have been dancing there. The place becomes dark, as they sleep there, because they are tired, when they have danced there.

Therefore, morning is (the time) when they send the children to the water, that the children may dip up (water) for them, that they may drink; for they are thirsty. Therefore, the children go early to dip up (water) for them, at the break of day, so that they may come to drink. For they are

1. The men are those, on the backs of whose heads the sun shines (literally, upon "the holes above the nape of their neck.").
2. They sleep at noon, because the women had bound on the drum for them, when the sun had just set.

thirsty. They are aware that they are tired. Therefore it does not seem as if they will be those to send the children to the water; for they feel at first that they are still tired. Therefore, it does not seem as if they will be those to send the children to the water. Because they are still sleeping there for a while; because they are still tired. Therefore, they do not seem as if they will be those to send the children to the water. Therefore, when they awake, they send the children to the water; when they feel that they have had their sleep out. Therefore, they awake. And then they send the children to the water. They speak to the children, they thus say to the children, that the children must quickly bring them water, that they may quickly come to drink. For they are thirsty.

PREPARATION OF THE FEATHER BRUSHES USED IN SPRINGBOK HUNTING.[1]

They roll the feather brushes, binding the ostrich feathers (the body feathers) upon the "Driedoorn" stick. They become numerous; and they (the Bushmen) pound red stones,[2] they paint[3], the feather brush sticks. And they make ready the (dried) skin of a springbok's chest; they thread little thongs[4]

1. I used to see my grandfather (*Tsatsi*) roll the feather brushes.
2. The red stones here meant, are ||*ka*; not *tto*. At the "Philadelphia Exhibition," in November, 1875, *Dia!kwain* recognized red hæmatite as ||*ka*.
3. Paint them red.
4. Thongs (they) are. The "children of thongs" (they) are. The Korannas call them *!Ya*.

into (it); and they put away the feather brushes. They put away the feather brushes; they dig ||*kuain*,[1] they roast (the stem of) the ||*kuain*, they lay the feather brushes over the ||*kuain*'s smoke, while the ||*kuain*'s smoke ascends into the feather brushes.

First, they dig[2] [with a stick pointed with horn], making a little hole; they put live coals into it. And they put ||*kuain* upon the live coals, while they wish that the ||*kuain* may smoke quietly, and not flame up; for the ||*kuain* would set the feather brushes on fire, if the fire were to flame up, if they (the stems) flamed up, when roasted.

They (the Bushmen) put the springbok skin[3] over (the fire); they put a stone upon the place where the feather brush sticks are for they intend that the smoke should only go out through the ostrich feathers.

1. Its stem is that which the people call ||*kuain*, because it does not a little smell. Therefore, the people smoke the feather brushes with it. The people call the stem of the !Ywa-kau, which is in the earth, ||*kuain*.
2. Men dig with sticks which have no stones (upon them); they are those with which men dig.
3. They turn the skin, into which the feather brushes have been put, upside down, over the hole into which the live embers and the ||*kuain* were put.

THE MARKING OF ARROWS.

The Bushmen are those who mark arrows,[1] while they wish that they may recognize the arrows, when they are shooting springbok at one place. And, when they are following the springbok spoor, when

1. All the arrows.

they are going along picking up the arrows they recognize the arrows. They say: "Thy arrow it seems to be, for, their mark is like this." Another man says: "Yes, my arrow is yonder." They again go to pick up this arrow. The other man says: "My arrow seems to be yonder; for their mark is like this."

|*kwae*[1] is that with which they make the marks. They put *tto* into (it), and they pound the *tto* together with the ||*kuae*; and the ||*kuae* becomes red on account of it; then, they mark the arrows with it.

1. They (the farmers) call it "Harpis." (Probably harpuis, * * * "resin.")

THE ADHESIVE SUBSTANCE USED BY THE BUSHMEN IN MARKING ARROWS.

It is |*kwae*[1]; it is ||*kuarri* juice. It is like a pumpkin, it is round. Its juice is white; it is like water. Its juice is not a little white; its whiteness resembles milk. It is poison.

We make an incision(?) (and) set it (the ||*kuwarri*) down; and then we hold a tortoise (shell) underneath it; because we wish its juice to be upon the tortoise (shell), that we may make ||*kuae* of it. And we warm (it) by the fire, making it hot; and we beat(?) it, when it is hot. Then, we beat(?), cooling it. And we take it up in this manner,[2] with a "Driedoorn" stick; we do in this manner to it, with the "Driedoorn" stick, as we make it round; while we think that we intend to make little springbok arrows.

1. The later spelling of this word has been followed in the translation, as probably more correct.
2. The narrator here imitated the manner of taking lip the |*kwae* by means of rolling it upon a stick.

MODE OF GETTING RID OF THE EVIL INFLUENCE OF BAD DREAMS.

My mother used to do in this manner, when she intended to go out to seek for food, when sho was about to start, she took a stone; (and) as she plunged the stone into the ashes of the fire, she exclaimed: "Rider(?) yonder!" while she wished that the evil things, about Which she had been dreaming, should altogether remain in the fire; instead of going out with her. For, if she did not act in this manner, they would go out with her. That place to which she went would not be nice; while she knew that she had dreamt of evil things which were not nice. Therefore, she acted in this manner; because she was aware that, if she went out with the dream which she had dreamt, her going out would not be fortunate.

The Bushman rice which she dug would not be favourable to her, because it was aware that she had dreamt evil things. Therefore, the Bushman rice would not be favourable to mamma; while the Bushman rice was aware that mamma had dreamt evil things; therefore, the Bushman rice would act in this manner about it.

CONCERNING TWO APPARITIONS.

We buried my wife in the afternoon. When we had finished burying her, we returned to the home of my sister, *Whai-ttu*,[1] and the other people, whence they had come forth. They had come to bury my wife with me; and we went away, crossing over the salt pan.

And we perceived a thing, which looked like a little child, as it sat upon the salt pan, seeming-is if it sat with its legs crossed over each other.

And my sister, *Whai-ttu*, spoke, she questioned us: "Look ye! What thing sits yonder upon the salt pan? It is like a little child." And *!kweiten-ta-||ken* [another sister] spoke, she asked us: "Look ye! Why is it that this thing is truly like a person? It seems as if it had on the cap which *Ddia!kwain*'s wife used to wear." And my sister, *Whai-ttu*, spoke, she answered: "Yes, O my younger sister! The thing truly resembles that which brother's wife was like." It did thus as we went along, it seemed as if it sat looking (towards) the place from which we came out.

And ||*ku-ang* spoke, she said: The old people used to tell me, that the angry people were wont to act thus, at the time when they took a person away, they used to allow the person to be in front of us, (so that) we might see it. Ye know that she really had a very little child, therefore, ye should allow us to look at the thing which sits upon this salt pan; it strongly resembles a person, its head is there,) like a person." And I spoke, I said: "Wait! I will do thus, as I return to my home, I will see, whether I shall again perceive it, as it sits."

And we went to their home. And we talked there, for a little while. And I spoke, I said to

1. *Whai-ttu* means "Springbok Skin".

them that they appeared to think that I did not wish to return (home); for the sun was setting. And I returned on account of it. I thought that I would go in the same manner as we had come; that I might, going along, look whether I should again perceive it, as it sat. Going along I looked at the place, where it had sat; because of thought that it might have been a bush. I saw that I did not perceive it, at the place where it had sat. And I agreed that it must have been a different kind of thing.

For my mothers used to tell me that, when the sorcerers are those who take us away, at the time when they intend to take us quite away, that is the time when our friend is in front of us, while he desires that we may perceive him, because he f eels that he still thinlis of us. Therefore, his outer skin[1] still looks at us, because he feels that he does not want to go away (and) leave us; for he insists upon coming to us. Therefore, we still perceive him on account of it.

My sister's husband, *Mansee*,[2] told us about it, that it had happened to him, when he was hunting about, as he was going along, he espied a little child, peeping at him by the side of a bush. And he thought: 'Can it be my child who seems to

1. That part of him (with) which he still thinks of us, is that with which he comes before us, at the time when the sorcerers are taking him away; that is the time when he acts in this manner. For, my mother and the others used to tell me, that they change(?) (when we die) we do as the last people do, themselves into a different thing.
2. My sister, |*a-kkumm*'s husband it was who told us, that he bad perceived a child who was afraid of him. It wanted to run away.

have run after me? It seems to have lost its way, while it seems to have followed me.' And *Mansse* thought: 'Allow me to walk nearer, that I may look at this child (to see) what child (it) be.'

And *Mansse* saw that the child acted in this manner, when the child saw that he was going up to it, that he might see what child it was, he saw that the child appeared as if it feared him. The child sat behind the bush; the child looked from side to side; it seemed as if it wanted to run away. And he walked, going near to it; and the child arose, on account of it. It walked away, looking from side to side; it seemed as if it wanted to run away.

And *Mansse* looked (to see) why it was that the child did not wish him to come to it; and the child seemed to be afraid of him.

And he examined the child; as the child stood looking at him. He saw that it was a little girl; he saw that the child was like a person. In other parts[1] (of it) it was not like a person; be thought that he would let the child alone. For a child who was afraid of him was here. And he walked on, while the child stood looking from side to side. And (as) the child saw that he went away from it, it came forward (near the bush), it sat down.

1. At one time, when he looked at it, it was not like a person; for, it was different looking, a different thing. The other part of it resembled a person.

THE JACKAL'S HEART NOT TO BE EATEN.

They (the Bushmen) feel that a little child is wont to be timid; therefore, the little child does not eat jackals' hearts; because the jackal is not a little afraid; for the jackal runs away.

The leopard is the one whose heart the little child eats; it which is not afraid; for, a little child becomes a coward from the jackal's heart, it fears immoderately (?).

Therefore, we do not give to a little child the jackal's heart; because we feel that the jackal is used to run away, when it has not (even) seen us; when it has only heard our foot rustle, it runs away, while it does not look towards (us).

Note added by the Narrator.

He (my grandfather, *Tssatssi*) had bought dogs from |*gappem-ttu*, and |*gappem-ttu* gave him a dog. And he took hold of the dog, he tied the dog up; and he took the dog away; holding the thong with which he had tied up the dog. He at first kept the dog tied up; and, when the dog had slipped his thong(?), he put it upon the scent(?), and the dog killed jackals.

He (my grandfather) skinned the jackals; and my grandmothers dressed the jackals' skins; they dressed them, they sewed them.

He again(?) killed(?) a jackal and an *Olocyon Lalandii*, he brought them (home), he skinned them.

And he made a kaross for |*gappem-ttu*, a jackals' kaross, while he put on the *Otocyon* kaross, the *Otocyon* skin.

And he took the kaross to |*gappem-ttu*, the jackals' kaross, while he felt that |*gappem-ttu* was the one who had given him the dog. Therefore, he made a kaross for i|*gappem-ttu*; while be made for |*gappem-ttu* an equivalent(?) for the dog; therefore, he gave the kaross to |*gappem-ttu*, and |*gappem-ttu* also gave him a pot, while he rewarded (?) my grandfather for the jackals' kaross. And my grandfather returned home.

Then my grandfather used to act in this manner, when he was boiling a jackal, he said: "Thou dost seem to think that we eat jackals' hearts? for, we become cowards (if we do so)." Therefore, we did not eat the jackals' hearts.

For, my grandfather used not to eat the jackal; he only boiled the jackal for his sons.

||HARA AND TTO.

||*hara*[1] is black; the people [having mixed it with fat] anoint their heads with it; while *tto* is red, and the people rub their bodies with it, when they have pounded it; they pound it, pound it, pound it, they rub their bodies with it. They pound ||*hara*, they anoint their heads, when they have first

1. A certain stone which is said to be boith hard and soft.

pounded the *tto*; they first rub their bodies with *tto*. And they pound ||*hara*, they anoint their heads. They anoint their heads very nicely, while they wish that their head's hair may descend (ie., grow long). And it becomes abundant on account of it; because they have anointed their heads, wishing that the hair may grow downwards, that their heads may become black with blackness, while their heads are not a little black.

And they return, when they come away from the other man, while they return to their home; when they have told the other person (the woman) about it, that the other person shall prepare [More] ||*hara* for them, as well as *tto*. For he (the man) also goes, (his) wife will go to dress bags for him, bags which he will also bring to the other man; while the other (man's wife) will also put aside ||*hara* for him, when the other (man) collects ||*hara*. And the other (man) comes to put aside ||*hara* for him; while she [the wife of the man who brought the bags] also dresses (and) puts away bags for the other; for, she has told the other (woman) that the other must also bring her ||*hara* and *tto*; for she has been to the other, and she will not be coming (soon again) to the other, for, the other must go to her; the other must go to receive the bags, when the other takes *tto* to her. Therefore, the other one also does so; she takes to the other *tto* and ||*hara*.

||*hara* sparkles; therefore, our heads shimmer, on account of it; while they feel that they sparkle, they shimmer. Therefore, the Bushmen are wont to say, when the old women are talking there: "That man, he is a handsome young man, on account of his head, which is surpassingly beautiful with the ||hara's blackness." They say, "Handsome young man" to him, "His head is surpassingly beautiful; for, his head is like the *!khi* tree.[1]

It is a tree which is in our country; it is the *!khi* tree; it is large; (it) is a great tree. They are not a little abundant in our country: the ||*Ukerri* tree and the *khi*.

1. The *!khi* tree bears berries; and has no thorns.

HOW TTO IS OBTAINED.

Tto is in the mountain, the *tto* mine; the people say that the *tto* mine is on the side of the mountain, the people say '*tto* mine' to it.

The people are afraid of it [that is, of the sorcerers who live by the mine], because the people are aware that people are there (sorcerers). They (the sorcerers) make a house[1] there. Theref ore, the people who intend to pound *tto*, rub themselves when they (go to) collect *tto*. And when they go to the *tto*, they throw stones at the *tto* mine, when they wish the sorcerers to hide themselves, that they may go undisturbed to work at the *tto*, while they feel that the sorcerers dwell at the *tto* mine. Therefore, they take up stones, they throw stones at the *tto* mine, when they wish the sorcerers to hide themselves, that they may go in peace[2] to work at the *tto*. And they go to work at the *tto, tto, tto*. They also get ||*hara*;[3] they put away the ||*hara* and the *tto*, and they return home.

1. The narrator thinks that their houses are small holes, like mouse-holes.
2. For, they would be ill, if the sorcerers saw them.
3. The ||*hara* mine [literally, "mouth" or "opening"] is in a different place; the *tto* mine is also in a different place.

SIGNS MADE BY BUSHMEN IN ORDER TO SHOW IN WHICH DIRECTION THEY HAVE GONE.

They (the Bushmen) are accustomed to act thus, when another man has gone away (and) does not return, they push their foot along the ground,[1] if they travel away; and they place grass[2] near the marks (they have made); and the other man does thus, when he returns, he comes (and) misses them at the house. He looks at the house, he looks (and) looks, he perceives the grass standing upright. And he goes to the grass, he looks at the grass. He also perceives the grass which stands yonder.[3]

And he exclaims: "The people must have travelled away to the water pool there." And he goes to the water, while he goes, looking (and) seeking for the people, (to see) whether the people have gone to dwell at that water.

And, he goes, ascending the water's hill;[4] he sits upon (it), that he may, sitting, look, look seeking for the huts. And he perceives the huts, as the huts stand white yonder. He sits, looking at them; the (smoke of the) fire[5] rises from the huts,[6] as he sits looking. And he exclaims: "The

1. They push their foot along the ground.
2. (They) stick grass into the bushes.
3. There are four pieces of grass, at a distance from each other, in the direction of the place to which the people have gone.
4. (It) is a hill, behind which the water is.
5. All the fires smoke.
6. The fire is outside.

house must be yonder!" And he arises, he goes to the house, and, returning, arrives) at home.

And the other people exclaim: "Our brother must be (the one who) comes yonder; for, he is the one who walks in this manner; for, a man of the place (he) is, he knows the water. He would do thus, when he came past (and) missed the house. He would come to the water which he knew. For, ye did say that he would lose his way,[1] when I said that we should travel away. Ye did say that he would lose his way, when I wished that we should travel away, although we had not told him about it that we should travel away; for, the water was gone. Therefore, we travelled away on account of it."

We are used also to reverse branches.[2] We thus place them, their green top is underneath, while the stump of the branch is uppermost. And we again, we go yonder to place that branch. And we draw our foot along the ground (making a mark), while we feel that we shall not again go to place another branch; because we altogether travel away.[3]

Therefore, the other man is wont to do thus, when he returns home (and) misses the house.

1. The Bushmen are those who say, | |gui !k'u, while the white men are those who say, "verdwall" (i.e. verdwalen, "to lose one's way").
2. Pierce it into the ground.
3. I feel that I used to see nay grandfather reverse (branches).
4. Four branches (and sometimes five) are said to be used; the first is placed opposite to the house, the next about fifty yards distant, the next a little further than that distance, the next rather more than double the previous distance, and, then, no more. At the last stick, the foot is drawn along the ground in the direction of the place to which they go, from the last stick; which leans in the same direction.

He looks (about), and he espies a branch; and he exclaims: "The folk must have travelled away to that little pool, for, this is why they have reversed (a branch), pointing in the direction of the place where the water is. I will go down(?) to the water, that I may go to look for the people's footprints at the water, at the place to which they seem to have gone to make a house,[1] (from which) they go to the water." And he goes to the water, he goes down(?) to the water. And he goes to look at the water, he espies the people's footpath, he takes it,[2] he follows it, follows it along to the house.

1. Seeking for food (to dig up) is one thing; making a house is different: "to dwell at a place."
2. The people's footpath is that which goes along.

A BUSHMAN, BECOMING FAINT FROM THE SUN'S HEAT WHEN RETURNING HOME, THROWS EARTH INTO THE AIR, THAT THOSE AT HOME MAY SEE THE DUST AND COME TO HELP HIM.[1]

A man is wont, when returning home, when he feels as if he should not reach home, he throws up earth (into the air), because he wishes that the, people at home may perceive the dust.

And the person who is looking out,[2] standing up to look out,—because she feels that the sun is not a little hot,—she stands up, she looks

1. Dying is that on account of which a person throws up earth (into the air).
2. (It) is the man's wife; while she feels that (her) husband has not returned; for, she sees that all the (other) people have returned home.

around.[1] And, as she stands looking around, she perceives the dust, she exclaims: "A person seems to be throwing up earth there!"

And the people run, run out[2] of the house, exclaiming: "His heart is that on account of which he throws up earth. Ye must run quickly, that ye may go to give him water quickly; for, (it) is his heart; the sun is killing him; (it) is his heart; ye must quickly go to give him water." While the people feel that all the people run to the man. They go, pouring (water), to cool the man with water.

And he first sits up,[3] to remove the darkness from his face; for, the sun's darkness resembles night.

These are not women's doings; for, men's doings they are.

They (the Bushmen) feel that they chase[4] things, chase the springbok; and it happens thus when they are tired by running, the sun is killing them

1. While she feels that the old man (her father) was the one who said: "My child! (?) thou art not standing up that thou mightst look around seeking for (thy) husband. The sun is really(?) very hot, for it did scorch me as I walked hither; as if it were not still morning, the sun did scorch me."
2. While they feel that they are numerous.
3. He was lying down, on account of his heart.
4. (To) run after a (wounded) springbok, to run after a springbok which we have shot. A wounded springbok they call: "a wounded thing(?)." A springbok, which is not wounded, they call: "a living springbok."

    People who are strong to bear the sun('s heat), they are those who chase the living (i.e. unwounded) springbok; they run after them through the sun, and the springbok vomit on account of it. And they turn the springbok, chasing, take the springbok to the house.

when they are tired. Then, they go staggering along, also (from) fatigue. The fatigue goes out, and they become cool. Then, they go staggering along, while they go along becoming cool, when they were previously hot; while they feel that they still perspire. Therefore, they go along staggering, widle they do not feel as if they should reach home; therefore, they go to sit down; they throw up earth (into the air); throw up earth for the people at home, while they wish that the people at home may perceive the dust.

DEATH.

The star does in this manner, at the time when our heart falls down, that is the time when the star also falls down; while the star feels that our heart falls over.[1] Therefore, the star falls down on account of it. For the stars know the time at which we die. The star tells the other people who do not know that we have died.

Therefore, the people act thus, when they have seen a star, when a star has fallen down, they say: "Behold ye! Why is it that the star falls down? We shall bear news; for a star falls down. Something which is not good appears to have occurred at another place; for the star tells us, that a bad thing has happened at another place."

1. As when something which has been standing upright, falls over on to its side.

The hammerkop[1] acts in this manner, when a star has fallen, it comes; when it flies over us, it cries.[2] The people say: "Did ye not hear the hammerkop, when the star fell? It came to tell us that our person is dead." The people speak, they say that the hammerkop is not a thing which deceives, for it would not come to our home, if it did not know; for, when it knows, then it comes to our home; because it intends to come and tell us about it, namely, that our person has died.

Therefore, mother and the others used,-if they heard a hammerkop, when it flew, going over us, to say: "Do thou go (and) plunge in, * * * for I know that which thou camest to tell me", while mother and the others said that the story, which it came to tell, should go into the Orange River's water, where the stars stand in the water. That is the place where its stories should go in. For mother and the others did not want to hear the story which it came to tell; for they knew that the hammerkop does in this manner at the time when a man dies, that is the time at which it comes to us, it tells us about it, that the man has died. For, mother and the others used to say,

211

1. Of this bird, the *Seopus umbrella*, or *Hammerkop*, the following description is given in "The Birds of South Africa" by E.L. Layard, Cape Town, 1867, p. 312.

   'The "*Hammerkop*" (literally, Hammerhead) is found throughout the colony, and all the way to the Zambezi, frequenting ponds, marshes, rivers, and lakes. It is a strange, weird bird, flitting about with great activity in the dusk of the evening, and preying upon frogs, small fish, &c. At times, when two or three are feeding in the same small pool, they will execute a singular dance, skipping round one another, opening and closing their wings, and performing strange antics.'

2. *Yak!* or *Yaak!* is the bird's cry, which it repeats twice.

that the hammerkop is a thing which lives at that water in which we see all things. Therefore, it knows what has happened; while it is aware that it lives at the water which is like a pool, in which we see all things; the things which are in the sky we see in the water, while we stand by the water's edge. We see all things, the stars look like fires which burn.

When it is night, when another man walks across, we see him, as he walks passing the water. It seems as if it were noonday, when he walks by the water. We see him clearly. The place seems as if it were midday as we see him walking along. Therefore, mother and the others said, that, when the hammerkop has espied in the water a person who has died, even though it be at a distance, when it knows that (he) is our relative, it flies away from this water, it flies to us, because it intends to go to tell us about it, that our relative has died. (It) and the star are those who tell us about it when we have not heard the news; for they are those who tell us about it, and when we have heard the hammerkop, we also perceive the star, we afterwards hear the news, when we have just perceived them; and we hear the news, wlien they have acted in this manner towards us.

For, mother and the others used to tell us about it, that girls are those whom the Rain carries off; and the girls remain at that water, to which the Rain had taken them, girls with whom the Rain is angry. The Rain lightens, killing them; they become stars, while their appearance has been changed. They become stars. For, mother and the others used to tell us about it, that a girl, when the Rain has carried her off, becomes like a flower[1] which grows in the water.

We who do not know are apt (?) to do thus when we perceive them, as they stand in the water, when we see that they are so beautiful; we think, 'I will go (and) take the flowers which are standing in the water. For they are not a little beautiful.' Mother and the others said to us about it, that the flower—when it saw that we went towards it,—would disappear in the water. We should think, 'The flowers which were standing here, where are they? Why is it that I do not perceive them at the place where they stood, here?' It would disappear in the water, when it saw that we went towards it; we should not perceive it, for it would go into the water.

Therefore, mother and the others said to—as about it, that we ought not to go to the flowers which we see standing in the water, even if we see their beauty. For, they are girls whom the Rain has taken away, they resemble flowers; for (they) are the water's wives, and we look at them, leaving them alone. For we (should) also be like them (in) what they do.

Therefore, mother and the others do in this manner with regard to their Bushman women, they are not willing to allow them to walk about, when the Rain comes; for they are afraid that the Rain also intends, lightening, to kill them. For the Rain is a thing which does in this manner when it rains

1. #*kamme*-ang's mother, |*abbe-ttu*, was the one who formerly told mamma about the flower which grows in the water; she said to mamma about it, that mamma seemed to think that she would not also become a flower, if she did not fear the Rain.

here, it smells our scent, it lightens out of the place where it rains. It lightens, killing us at this place; therefore, mother and the others told us about it, that when the Rain falls upon us (and) we walk passing through the Rain, if we see that the Rain lightens in the sky we must quickly look towards the place where the Rain lightens; the Rain, which intended to kill us by stealth. It will do in this manner, even if its thunderbolts[1] have come near us, (if) we look towards (the place where it has lightened), we look, making its thunderbolts turn back from us; for our eye also shines like its thunderbolts. Therefore, it also appears to f ear our eye, when it feels that we quickly look towards it. Theref ore, it passes over us on account of it; while it feels that it respects our eye which shines upon it. Therefore, it goes over us; it goes to sit on the ground yonder, while it does not kill us.

1. Black, pointed, shining stones, which only come from the sky when it lightens. They disturb the ground where they fall. They are called !*khwa* !*kweiten* (the Rain's thunderbolts).

THE RELATIONS OF WIND, MOON, AND CLOUD TO HUMAN BEINGS AFTER DEATH.

The wind does thus when we die, our (own) wind blows; for we, who are human beings, we possess wind; we make clouds, when we die. Therefore, the wind does thus when we die, the wind makes dust, because it intends to blow, taking away our footprints, with which we had walked about while we still had nothing the matter with

us; and our footprints, which the wind intends to blow away, would (otherwise still) lie plainly visible. For, the thing would seem as if we still lived. Therefore, the wind intends to blow, taking away our footprints.

And, our gall,[1] when we die, sits in the sky; it sits green in the sky, when we are dead.

Therefore, mother was wont to do thus when the moon lying down came, (when) the moon stood hollow. Mother spoke, she said: "The moon is carrying people who are dead. For, ye are those who see that it lies in this manner; and it lies hollow, because it is killing itself (by) carrying people who are dead. This is why it lies hollow. It is not a | | *k'auru*; for, it is a moon of badness(?).[2] Ye may (expect to) hear something, when the moon lies in this manner. A person is the one who has died, he whom the moon carries, Therefore, ye may (expect to) hear what has happened, when the moon is like this."

The hair of our head will resemble clouds, when we die, when we in this manner make clouds. These things are those which resemble clouds; and we think that (they) are clouds. We, who do

1. Mother, she used to tell me, that it (thus) happens to us if we sit in the shade when the place is not particularly warm, when it is (only) moderately warm, (and) we feel that the summer seems as if it would be hot. We think: 'Allow me to sit for a little in the shade under the bush; for the sun's eye is not a little hot; I will sit a little while in the shade;' (then) we make clouds; our liver goes out from the place where we are sitting in. the shade, if the place is not hot. Therefore, we make clouds on account of it. For, when it is really summer, then we (may) sit in the shade.
2. Possibly, "of threatening."

not know, we are those who think in this manner, that (they) are clouds. We, who know, when we see that they are like this, we know that (they) are a person's clouds; (that they) are the hair of his head. We, who know, we are those who think thus, while we feel that we seeing recognize the clouds, how the clouds do in this mauner form themselves.

APPENDIX.

A. FEW !KUNG TEXTS.

THE DOINGS OF |XUE ARE MANY.

The works of |*Xue* are many, and were not one, but many; and my father's father, *Karu*, told me about |*Xue*'s doings, for |*Xue*'s works are numerous.

VARIOUS TRANSFORMATIONS OF |XUE

1. |XUE AS !NAXANE.

(When) the sun rose, |*Xue* was *!naXane*; the birds ate |*Xue*; |*Xue* was *!naXane*. The sun set, (and) |*Xue*, was |*Xue*; and lay down and slept. The night fell, and |*Xue* lay down, (he) slept; the place was dark; and the sun rose, and |*Xue* was another (kind of) *!naXane*, a large (kind of) *!naXane*, which is a tree. And the night fell, (and) |*Xue* was not a tree, and was |*Xue*, and lay down.

2. FURTHER CHANGES OF FORM.

The sun rose, and |*Xue* was a *dui*;[1] and the sun set, and |*Xue* was an Omuherero and lay down; and the sun rose, and |*Xue* was |*Xue*, and went into another country and was a *sha'o*[2]; and the sun

1. The flower of the *dui* is light-coloured; its fruit is green; another day, (when) its fruit has ripened, its fruit is red.
2. The *shao* is a tall tree, like the *!kuni* (palm?).

set, and |*Xue* was a Makoba, and lay down; and the sun rose and |*Xue* was a |*naXane*.[1]

1. (One kind of) *!naXane* lies upon the earth; another (kind of) *!naXane* is a tree. The *!naXane* are numerous. The fruit of the tree *!naXane* is yellowish. The fruit of the tree *!naXane* is large; and the ground *!naXane* fruit is small, and resembles the |*kui* fruit, is red, is small, and abundant.

3. |XUE AS A ||GUI TREE AND AS A FLY.

The sun set, and |*Xue* was |*Xue*, and lay upon the ground, and slept, was alone, and lay upon the ground and slept. And the sun rose, and |*Xue* awoke and . . . and stood up, and saw the sun,-a little sun,-and was | |*gui*, and was a tree.

And his wife saw the | |*gui*, and went to the | |*gui*, and went to take hold of a |*gui* fruit, and the | |*gui* vanished; and |*Xue* was a fly. And his wife laid herself upon the earth, and cried about the |*gui*, and died. And |*Xue* was a fly, and settled upon the grass.[1] And his wife lay down upon the earth, and cried about the | |*gui*[2]

1. And he settled upon the grass, and the grass broke. The naine of the grass is *goo*.
2. The | |*gui* is a tree. People eat the | |*gui*, the | |*gui* fruit. People do not put the | |*gui* into a pot, but eat it raw. The | |*gui* has thorns.

4. |XUE AS WATER AND AS OTHER THINGS. IN HIS OWN FORM, HE RUBS FIRE AND DIES.

|*Xue* was water; and the water was (in) the shadow of the tree. And the wood pigeons ate the fruit of the |*kui* And |*Xue* was a lizard[1] and lay in the dead leaves of the |*kui*. And (he) saw the wood pigeons, and was water[2] And the wood pigeons saw the water, and settled upon the water's edge. And |*Xue* worked large grass, like reeds, and it took hold of a wood pigeon. And the wood pigeons came to drink (lit. to eat) water, and the grass I came near, and bit the wood pigeon's bill, and the wood pigeon cried out; and the other wood pigeons flew away.

And |*Xue* was |*Xue* and rose up, and took hold of the wood pigeon, and plucked out the wood pigeon's feathers, and put the wood pigeon's feathers in his head, and lay upon the ground. And the water vanished, and he was and put the wood pigeon's feathers in his head, and lay upon the ground. And (he) put the wood pigeon's body into the hot embers, and lay down. And continued to lie down, and arose, and went to take out the wood pigeon's body from the fire.

And (he) ate the wood pigeon, and heard Ovahereró, and arose. And went to the Ovahereró, and the Ovahereró saw him. And he hid himself on the ground. The Ovahereró came to search for him, to search for him, (and) did not see him. For (he) was little, and was a |*nu-erre*;[4] and a little Omuhereró boy saw the |*nu-erre* upon a bush, and

---

1. This lizard (called also *ggoru* and *nggoru* by my !*kung* informants and |*hai-@pua* by |*hang#kass'o*) appears to be the comnion Gecko.
2. (He) was not a large (piece of) water, but (?) was a little water, a water hole.

222

3. |*Xue* was a grass which is (called) *go*, and (is) small; and bit the wood pigeon. Large grass, which is (called) reeds, took hold of the wood pigeon; and was |*Xue*.
4. A (certain) little bird.

he saw the Ovahereró, and cried out.¹ And was the Bushman's eye water and fell upon the ground. And he said: "Ye-he! Ye-he! Ye-he!" And the Omuhereró heard, and sought for him, sought for him, sought f or him, and did not see him, and (he, |*Xue*) flew away.

And (he, |*Xue*)² flew, coming to his mother's country, and saw his father, and was not a |*nu-erre* but was |*Xue*, and died.³ And his father went to him, and came to look at him, and he was dead. And his father went away, and he was not dead, and was and rose up. He called to his father: "My father! O!" and his father called to him, and said: "My child! O!" and he called to his father once, and cried out: "#*no!* #*no!*" and came to his mother's country.

And his father saw him and stealthily approached him. And he heard his father. And (he) saw his father, and died; and was a lizard, and lay down, lay down upon the ground.

And his father saw him, and said: "It is my child, |*Xue*! for it is not another person, but is my child; and (he) saw me, and died. And (he) was rubbing sticks (to make) fire⁴; and saw me, and died; and is not another person, but is my child, and is |*Xue*. For, I went (?) away to my country, and did not see my child; and today,

1. And (he) cried: "*Tsuai! tsuai! tsuai!*" (Two) Ovahereró children saw him; for be was a |*nu-erre*.
2. |*Xue* was a |*nu-erre*, and cried out. He was not one |*nu-erre* but was many |*nu-erre*.
3. He was [now] not many |*nu-erre*, bat was one |*nu-erre*, and went to his mother's country.
4. He carried over his shoulder a little bag, the skin of an antelope, a female antelope's skin.

I saw my child, and my child was rubbing fire, little sticks' fire;¹ and my child rubbed fire, and saw me, and died. And is |*Xue*; and is not another person, but is |*Xue*. I am afraid of my child, for my child is dead.

"I go to my country; and my country is far away, and (during) many moons I go to my country, (and) do not see my country; my country is far distant. And, today, I see my child, for my child is and makes fire, little sticks' fire, and eats |*shana*,² and rubs fire, and his

223

hands hurt (him), and he cries, and sees me, and dies; for I am |*Xe-*||*n'u* and my child, |*Xue*, sees me, and dies; and I am afraid of my child. I go away to my country, my country that(?) is far distant.

"And my child is another person; I see my child. And (I) wear in my head wood pigeons' feathers; and my child saw me, my head with wood pigeons' feathers, many wood pigeon feathers, for they(?) were two wood pigeons. And, today, I am afraid of my child, and (I) go to my (own) country."

And (he) went to his (own) country; the name of his country is ||*noa*, it is a mountain, a large mountain. And he went away to his (own) country.

1. The tree's name was |*n'au-*|*kumm*, and (he had) two sticks; the fire stick (i.e., the one which he held in his hands) was long, small, and long, like a reed. The other (fire) stick lay on the ground; for he had laid (it) the other stick upon grass; he rubbed fire, the fire fell upon the grass; and he took up the fire (i.e., the grass), he blew the fire.
2. *Tshana* is the name of a tall fruit-bearing tree. The fruit of it is eaten raw.

PRAYER TO THE YOUNG MOON.[1]

    Young Moon!
    Hail, Young Moon!
    Hail, hail,
    Young Moon!

Young Moon! speak to me!

    Hail, hail,
    Young Moon!

Tell me of something.

    Hail, hail!
    When the sun rises,
    Thou must speak to me,
    That I may eat something.

Thou must speak to me about a little thing,

    That I may eat.
    Hail, hail,
    Young Moon!

1: When (?) we see the moon [*!nanni* elsewhere explained], we say *!ka!karrishe*; we sound the male antelope's horn.
    We call the small moon *!ka!karrishe*; (but) women call (it) *!ka!karibe*.

THE TREATMENT OF THIEVES.

If a *!kung* woman steals, her father and her mother being (still) there, we take hold of her, we give her to her mother and her father; and they all go away from their place. Her stolen thing, we take it, we run, we give (it) to the other person, run to give to the other person the other person's thing. And we say to the other person: "My wife stole your thing which is here; your nice thing here, my wife stole. And I have given (back) my wife to her father and her mother. For, my wife stole the nice thing here."

And the other person hears, and objects (saying):

"No; kill thy wife." And, we hear, (and) object (saying): "No; I do not listen to you, and will not kill my wife; for, my wife has gone away, has gone to her father and her mother; and is far away; and has gone to her country; and I will not kill my Wife."

And the others cry, and we hear; and our hearts ache, and-we go away; we say to the other people: "We go away; come, that I may kill my wife, kill my father-in-law, kill my mother-in-law, kill my . . ."[1]

On the day that the woman took the thing, we see the thing, we take the thing. The woman says to us: "My husband, look at my nice thing, here, which I stole."[2] And we hear; and we say:

1. Another relation.
2. A *!kung* woman is not afraid.

"My wife, give me thy thing, that I may look (at it)." And (we) persuade her; and she takes (it) and gives (it) to us. And we take (it), and put (it) into our bag; and she cries (saying): "Give me my thing, oh dear! My husband! give me my thing, oh dear!" And we refuse (saying): "No, my wife, I will not listen to thee; for, the other person would kill me; and I will give the other person the other person's thing. My wife! I will not listen to thee, for thou dost (try to) persuade me (in vain)."[1]

If a woman steals another person's thing, (and) returns to her husband, (and) her husband sees the other person's thing, his heart aches, and he kills her; he altogether kills his wife.[2]

Another man (*i.e.*, his father) says to him: "No; do not quite kill thy wife."[3] And, he objects (saying): "No; I object to stealing; and my heart aches; and I will kill my wife; leave off talking to me; today ye must fear me."

A female child, if her mother is dead and the female child is an only child, goes to another person's hut. Another day, if she steals, the other person into whose hut she went (to live) takes her, (and) gives her to the other person, the other (from

1. Should the father be dead, and the mother alive, the woman, who stole, is still taken and given back to the latter. And, should she be an old offender, the mother is said to give her, through a son, to another person, to be burned to death.
2. He shoots with an arrow, killing his wife; he shoots, killing his wife with a |*nubbo* (a particular kind of arrow).
3. Meaning, that he may beat her.

whom she stole, the other people kill her altogether; (they) put her in a hut, and burn, killing her with fire; and she dies altogether; and the other people return home.

They say to the people, to the people who gave them the girl who stole, they, (who) killed the girl, they say: "We have burning, killed the girl with fire, put the girl into a hut, and burning killed the girl. Leave off reproaching us about the girl." And the. other people object (saying): "No; we are not scolding you; for, we object (to stealing); for this[1] girl stole; and we do not scold you; for, we hear, and our hearts are glad."

If a man steals, we kill (him), we shoot, killing him (with) arrows,[2] and do not put him into the fire; but, kill him altogether with arrows. It is only a woman (whom) we burn, burn, putting (her) into the fire.

If a child steals, we merely scold the child;[3] and do not kill the child.

Another day, when the child has grown up, if it steals, we object, we kill the child;[4] give the child to other persons, and they kill it altogether.

1. We fear her name, and do not utter her name; (but) merely mention her.
    We fear the people whom we kill, on account of their spirits.

2. Many arrows, not a single arrow; the arrows of many persons; many persons shoot at him.
3. For, we respect the stealing of a little child.
4. We fear its name, and call it "child". Those persons whom we kill altogether, we fear their naraes; we do not utter their names.

If another woman comes into our hut (and) her child steals a thing of ours, (if) her child eats our food, (and) we see, we take it, and we take its mother, we give them to other people,[1] (and) the other people put them into the fire, and burn, burn, killing them with fire; (and) return (and) say to us: "We have, burning, killed the two people with fire." We hear; we say: "Yes; we object to stealing." And (we) are silent.[2] And they say: "We have burnt the two persons; ye must not scold (us)." Our hearts are glad,[3] and we sing. And (we) say to them: "We . . . object to stealing; and fear stealing; and do not steal." And those[4] (who killed the woman) hear; and (one) says: "Yes."[5]

And we give them a male elephant's tusk; and they go away to their home. And, another day, they give (it) to the Makoba. And the Makoba give them one bull, with Indian Hemp; and they give to us; and we kill, and eat (it) up; and they return to their home; and we speak nicely to them (saying): "Return ye to your dwelling; give us Indian Hemp; do not give us the bull alone; we object to one thing (only); we do not eat one thing; for, we eat two things." And they hear, and assent (to us); and they return to their home.

And we eat up the bull; and they say to us:

1. (They) are not strangers, but, are our other people (of the same place).
2. It is not many of us, but, one of us (who) speaks to him (to the other person).
3. Our many hearts are glad.
4. They (are) many.
5. Many other people listen, displeased; and one person assents, and says: "Yes."

"Ye have eaten up the bull; give us an elephant's tusk." And we hear; and our hearts are glad. The sun arises, and we return to our dwelling.[1] And come, telling the other people who are at our dwelling-our people-we say to them: "Give ye an elephant's tusk to the people." And the others, who are our people, hear; and we give them Indian Hemp.

1. When we have eaten up the bull, (we) go to their dwelling, to seek Indian Hemp; and they give us Indian Hemp.

THE FOUR PIECES OF WOOD CALLED |XU[1], USED FOR DIVINING PURPOSES.

The !kung women respect these things, (they) do not take hold (of them). Men take hold (of them). A small !kung child, who is a little girl, does not take hold of this thing; for (she) respects (it). For, her mother says to her: "This thing, thou must respect, my mother." And the child listens, (and) respects the thing; but a little male child does not fear the thing, (and) takes hold of the thing, (and) carries, carries the thing to his father.

And his father puts down[2] the thing upon the ground, and (the child) does not see (or look at) the thing, he goes away. For his father objects

1. The |Xu is a set of four pieces of wood, two "male" and two "female ". Spoons are also made from the wood of the same tree. The narrator described it as follows:—
    The name of the tree is !ke; and (it) is a food tree; (it) is not a mere tree. (It is) one tree, (from) which we make the thing (i.e., the set of !Xu).
    By the Makoba, the !Xu is called |nu|num. Their name for the fruit of the !ke tree is kanzuai.
2. (When putting down) one thing, I say ||ning, (when putting down) several things, I say ||ning-a.

(to his looking on, and says): "Go, my father!"[1] The child laughs, and runs off, goes to his mother, (and) says to his mother: "My mother! give water." For the child ran, coming (and) saying to his mother:

Give my father water."

And his mother took water (from the pot) with a gourd(?), the skin of food; and gave her child water; and her child carried the (vessel of) water in his hands, carried water to his father. And the water (vessel) fell, and (the water) poured upon the ground; and he (the boy) saw, and cried out: "My father! the water pours down, oh dear! My father! the water pours down, oh dear!" And his father heard him, and ran, coming to take hold of him. And (he) beat his child, broke off a little stick, and beat his child; and the little stick was a *shana*. And his son's speech was this (?): "My father! leave off beating me! oh dear! My father! leave off beating me! oh dear! My father! leave off striking me! oh dear! My father! leave off striking me! oh dear!"

And the people[2] took hold of him, his mother came to take hold of him (saying): "My mother! my child! oh dear! My mother! my child! oh dear! My mother! my husband is striking my child, oh dear!"

His (the child's) father came and took (his) quiver, and drew out an arrow, and put his arrow upon his bow; and the people (ie., the women) called out. For, he took aim at his wife with (two)

arrows; for his arrows were a |*nubbo*, and a ||*Xi*.[3]

1. (He) caressed (?) his child; for his child was a little boy.
2. (They) were not men, but were women.
3. He aimed at his wife with two arrows (one after the other).

And his wife cried, and avoided the arrow. And (she) cried; and his wife's mother cried: "My mother! my son-in-law takes aim at my daughter with two arrows, oh dear!" And (she) fell down, and lay upon the ground, and cried; and the people (many other women) came (and) took hold of her, and said to her: "Do not cry!" And she refused (saying): "No! my son-in-law aims at my daughter with two arrows, oh dear!" And the people took hold of her; and she would not listen to the people, and refused.

TO BEAT THE GROUND (WITH A STONE).

The *!kung* beat a stone upon the ground. My father's mother beat a stone upon the ground. She said: "Fall into the water ! Fall into the water!" And the thing (the lightning?) fell into the water.

A man does not beat a stone upon the ground. A woman beats a stone upon the ground.

My (*Tamme*'s) father's mother was *Ng-||na*. My mother's father was Little *Tamme*; and my mother's mother was *!karo-||n'a*. My father's father's father was Great *Tamme*.

SNAKES, LIZARDS, AND A CERTAIN SMALL ANTELOPE, WHEN SEEN NEAR GRAVES, TO BE RESPECTED.

A snake which is near a grave, we do not kill, for, (it) is our other person, our dead person, the dead person's snake.[1] And we do not kill (it); for (we) respect it. And (if, during) many days, we see it, we do not kill (it); looking (at it), (we) let it alone.

Another day, (if) we see a lizard, we f ollow the lizard's spoor; (if) the lizard has gone to the earth (grave?) of our other person, we respect the lizard, (we) do not kill the lizard, (we) let the lizard alone.

(When) we see an antelope,[2] an antelope (which is) near our other person's place, that place where our other person has died, we respect the antelope; for, the antelope is not a mere antelope. Its legs(?) seem(?) small, it is the person who has died, and is a spirit antelope. It is a male antelope; it is not a female antelope.

1. (When) our "other one", (who) is a man, dies, he becomes (?) a snake; and his snake is a spirit. A snake bites him, he dies, he is a snake.

    When a woman just dies, the woman has no snake. If a snake bites a woman, (and) the woman dies, the woman is a snake. If a woman merely dies, her sprit is a mere spirit.

    When a man dies, his "other" is a mere spirit; his "other" is a snake; near his earth (grave?); and his mere spirit goes away.

    If an elephant kills him, (he) becomes (?) one kind of snake; (he) is a #*ne-ko*, and is black; he is not a different kind of snake; for his heart aches.

2. At the Cape Town Museum, a very small kind of buck (the name of which the Curator did not know) was recognized as the |*ou* by my informants. It had been, I believe, brought from Damaraland or its neighbourhood.

    With regard to the above belief, it may also be mentioned that, on one occasion, I saw a snake close to the coping of a burial place; and showed it to !*nanni*, expecting him to destroy it. He merely looked at it in rather a strange way, and allowed it to depart uninjured; saying something about its being near a grave; which, at the time, I did not clearly understand—ED.

A CERTAIN SNAKE, WHICH, BY LYING UPON ITS BACK, ANNOUNCES A DEATH IN THE FAMILY; AND WHICH MUST NOT, UNDER THESE CIRCUMSTANCES, BE KILLED.

The ǀǀhing[1] (is) a serpent of our country. (If, when) we strike it, it does in this manner with its belly,[2] it

1. A. long, light-coloured snake, which does not bite, and is timid.
2. That is, turns the under side of its body upwards.

gives us its belly, we fear it, and go away, and return home; while (we) do not kill[1] it. For (we) let (it) alone; and it lies, lies, lies; arises, (and) goes away altogether.

And, another day, (if) we see it (and) it does not give us its belly, we beat it, we kill it altogether, and throw (it) altogether away; (we) do not keep (it) [do not eat it].[2]

Another day, (when) it sees us, (as) we approach it, approach it, approach it, (and) reach it, (and) it gives us its belly, we are afraid, we do not kill it, we run away.

Another day, we see it, (when) it is in the water—tree water[3]- we are near it, we think that we will drink water, we see its body, (when) it is in the water, (and) it sees us, it quickly(?) goes out of the water, and lies upon the ground. We think that we will strike it, (and) it gives us its belly, we turn back, we go away, and it alone lies (there).

And (if) a woman comes (and) the woman sees it, (she) unloosens (her) skin necklace, and (gently) lays (it) down; and it turns,[4] and lays its belly upon the earth. And the woman kills it, and throws it away.

(If) another person dies, (and) we have not heard his news,[5] (and) we see the ||*hing* turning its belly towards us, we are afraid of the ||*hing*, and cry.

1. And (we) tell the people who are at home, and say: "I saw a ||*hing*, and struck the ||*hing*, and the ||*hing* objected, and gave me its belly; and I was afraid of the ||*hing*, and did not kill the |*hing*. but ran away." And many women hear, (and) cry.
2. And, another day, (when) it lies nicely [not turning up its belly at us, in a hollow manner, while it lies on its back], we skin it, and throw away its flesh; and keep its skin; give the Makoba its skin.
3. Namely, that which is in the hollow of a tree.
4. It sees the woman, it does thus with its belly. It sees the woman's skin necklace, it is afraid; for the woman has worked the necklace with plenty of fat; and (it) smells good; its scent being powerful (*lit.* "long ", *i.e.*, reaching a long way)
5. The words ||*numm* and #*nua* both mean "news", "tidings".]

BIBLIOBAZAAR

The essential book market!

Did you know that you can get any of our titles in large print?

Did you know that we have an ever-growing collection of books in many languages?

Order online:
www.bibliobazaar.com

Find all of your favorite classic books!

Stay up to date with the latest government reports!

At BiblioBazaar, we aim to make knowledge more accessible by making thousands of titles available to you- *quickly and affordably*.

Contact us:
BiblioBazaar
PO Box 21206
Charleston, SC 29413